RICHARD "BUGMAN" FAGERLUND

My Path to the Bugman

With an Earth-Friendly Guide to Pest Management For Your Home and Garden

WHO chains YOU PUBLISHING

Published by Who Chains You Publishing
P.O. Box 581
Amissville, VA 20106

www.WhoChainsYou.com
www.AsktheBugman.com

ISBN-13: 978-1-946044-03-7
ISBN-10: 1-946044-03-2

Printed in the United States of America

First Edition

ﺒﺠﺳ

I DEDICATE THIS BOOK TO THE ELIMINATION OF PESTICIDES FROM SOCIETY AND EVERYONE WHO SUPPORTS THAT EFFORT, FOR PESTICIDES HAVE INDEED BECOME A DESTRUCTIVE FORCE FOR OUR PLANET. I DEDICATE THIS BOOK TO ALL THE CHILDREN IN THE WORLD WHO HAVE BEEN HARMFULLY IMPACTED BY PESTICIDES THROUGH NO FAULT OF THEIR OWN. I ALSO DEDICATE THIS BOOK TO ALL OF THE ANIMAL RESCUES AROUND THE WORLD; TO THOSE WHO STAND FOR ANIMALS, AND TO THOSE WHO CARE FOR ANIMALS. AND, AT THE RISK OF SOUNDING LIKE A FLOWER CHILD, I DEDICATE THIS BOOK TO PEACE, LOVE AND HAPPINESS EVERYWHERE...FOR WE HAVE FAR TOO LITTLE OF THESE THINGS.

OTHER BOOKS AND SCHOLARLY WORKS
BY RICHARD "BUGMAN" FAGERLUND

Books:

Ask the Bugman
The Bugman on Bugs

Scholarly Papers:

Mackay, W. P., and R. Fagerlund. 1997.
"Range expansion of the red imported fire ant, Solenopsis invicta Buren (Hymenoptera: Formicidae), into New Mexico and extreme West Texas." Proceedings of the Entomological Society of Washington 99:758-759.

Fagerlund, R.; Ford, P. L.; Brown, T.; Polechla, P. J., Jr. 2001.
New records for fleas (Siphonaptera) from New Mexico with notes on plague-carrying species. Southwestern Naturalist. 46: 94-95.

Ford, Paulette L.; Fagerlund, Richard A.; Duszynski, Donald W.; Polechla, Paul J. 2004.
Fleas and lice of mammals in New Mexico. Gen. Tech. Rep. RMRS-GTR-123. Fort Collins, CO: U.S. Department of Agriculture, Forest Service, Rocky Mountain Research Station. 57 p.

TABLE OF CONTENTS

CHAPTER ONE

THE BEGINNING...OF MY OBSESSION WITH
ALL THINGS CRAWLY AND SLITHERY? PROBABLY

I can't say for sure when I first discovered a love for bugs and other beings often termed "undesirable" by many; or the urge to protect them, to understand them, to work with them in a way that would respect their rights to exist whenever possible and encourage my fellow human beings to see them as more than just pests.

I do know that it couldn't have been before March 13, 1943, when I came into this world at Kings County Hospital in

Brooklyn, New York, born to Gunvor and Frederick Mosher. My biological father ran off when I was very young, so I know little to nothing about him, or what part of me might be a reflection of his gene pool. Mom met my future stepfather, Aldur Fagerlund, at Radio City Music Hall, fell in love, and married him in November of 1946, when I was just three years old.

Shortly thereafter, we moved to Sandy Creek, New York, which sits right next to Lake Ontario. We spent only a single year there, as the winters proved to be too cold for mom, and dad had to supplement his farming income by building things for other people. I remember him working on a roller rink and doing side carpentry for farmers and dairymen on the barter system. He grew corn, which Mom canned and we ate…all winter long.

Even though today I follow a vegan diet out of respect for the animals and a belief that it makes one healthier (and at my age I need all the health-perks I can get), as a child I never thought too much about where my next meal was coming from. I just hoped that it came.

We bought a young bull that dad was going to breed and make money from—until it picked him up and threw him over the fence. I clearly remember seeing that to this day, and I was only four years old. Talk about your early childhood animal trauma! From this one episode, and even at such a young age, I developed a healthy respect for the power of those beings we humans sought to control.

We also raised an adorable baby calf that would follow mom around and chew on her sweater, so in that one year on the farm I was exposed to both the positive and the negative sides of animal rearing.

I remember one incident that took place in Sandy Creek

that had a major impact on my life. I was about five years old and playing outside when my dad opened the cellar door and screamed. I ran over just as he grabbed a shovel and killed a small snake with it. Later on I would realize it was a garter snake, which aren't harmful to humans at all.

I asked my dad why he killed it, and I'll never forget his response: "because it's a snake and snakes have to be killed."

That didn't make any sense to me even at that young age. I thought of the incident often, so when I got to high school I decided to make use of the library and find out why snakes were so evil.

Instead, I found out the truth—that snakes are beneficial animals and do not need to be killed. After that I loved snakes and I'd go out and catch them and bring them home whenever I could, much to my dad's chagrin. I got really involved in herpetology and studied it almost my entire life, later also developing an interest in entomology, which I made into a career.

Of course, many experiences in my early years had nothing to do with bugs or snakes, and were simply life in mid-twentieth century America. But they all shaped me into the man I later became, for better or worse.

My mom became pregnant again with my sister Linda, and when spring 1948 came we moved to a Brooklyn basement apartment, a BIG difference from life on the farm. There we stayed until 1952 when my brother David was born, at which point we needed a bigger place, so we picked up and moved to North Massapequa on Long Island. Dad got work in the steel construction industry, and I remember him working on Penn Station and Radio City Music Hall, to name just two of the large jobs he'd become part of. I'm not sure his work life was any easier than on the farm, but we seemed to have an easier time making ends meet at least.

I would end up graduating from West Babylon High School in 1961, where we'd made yet another move to a few years earlier. I actually graduated with Geraldo Rivera, my claim to fame, who lived close to us in West Babylon—our parents were friends.

I didn't know what to do with myself after I graduated high school; I had no plan for my life, and there was nothing that brought excitement as a career option. The thought of going into construction like my father didn't appeal to me, and there was no money for college. So I up and joined the army.

When I enlisted I weighed a measly 138 lbs., next to nothing for a man of my height. I was sent to basic training in Fort Dix, New Jersey for eight weeks, where my drill sergeant, Sgt. Butler, told me I didn't have a chest to speak of, but they would fix that. And they sure did—with lots of pushups and pull-ups, the old-fashioned way. Apparently it worked, because when I left the army years later I weighed in at a healthy 180 lbs.

After basic training I was sent to signal school in Ft. Gordon, Georgia, where I trained as a radio operator before getting transferred to Schofield Barracks in Hawaii in early 1962. I was assigned to the 125th Signal Battalion, 25th Infantry Division, and spent some time in Southeast Asia with them prior to the Viet Nam war. Although I didn't hate being a radio operator, I don't remember feeling any kind of affinity with the career field choice, and would later leave it given the chance.

Like everyone of a certain age, I can remember exactly where I was on November 22, 1963 when President Kennedy was assassinated—I was loading a truck in Schofield Barracks and our company was getting ready to go out into the field. Everything on the base came to a halt, as we all congregated in front of the TVs in our barracks to watch the horrible news.

CHAPTER TWO

DRINKING SNEAKS UP ON ME

Like so many of the enlisted folks of the time, I started drinking beer with my fellow soldiers shortly after I left basic training. My first visit to a bar was when I was in radio school and stationed at Ft. Gordon, Georgia, and it quickly became a weekly habit. A large percentage of our classmates and myself spent a lot of time at clubs, drinking and acting crazy. We were young and full of ourselves, and thought we were invincible.

I quickly proved that was not the case, when I got arrested for the first time while stationed at Ft. Gordon for public intoxication as I staggered back to the fort after the bars had closed. I'd assume I wasn't the only one doing that exact same thing, as so many of us took to drinking heavily in those days, but apparently I was chosen as 'special' that night.

When I left Ft. Gordon to travel to my duty station in Hawaii, we boarded a train to Chicago, Illinois, and then another train to San Francisco, California. While on the train we had to obey the drinking laws of each state as we passed through. I was only 18 at the time, so I was able to drink in most states, only having to stop when we got to Utah. Heck, you weren't even allowed to smoke in Utah until you were 21! But as soon as we got out of Utah and entered Nevada, we were able to hit the bar car again.

From San Francisco, we flew to Hawaii and were allowed to drink on the plane—as you can imagine, I was roaring drunk when we landed in Honolulu. I was so smashed I couldn't even find the army jeep waiting to pick us up.

At the time, these crazy antics seemed like just young soldiers blowing off steam, but in reality I was taking my first steps toward alcoholism, and it's doubtful that I was alone in doing so.

When I wasn't working on base, I spent much of my time in one of the many local dives nearby. On occasion, I went to Honolulu and got a tattoo. Tattoos were pretty cheap then, and all the army guys got them, so I did too. I remember the most expensive one I got was $8.00. Compared to today's prices? Astounding!

Of course, I got most of my ink done while under the influence, but I made it a point to get one sober to see if it was painful. It was. I resolved to never get another tattoo unless I was "beyond the point of feeling pain," and I didn't.

On one occasion, a friend and I left a bar in Wahiawa and walked back to the base. We "got tired" and decided to rest in an unlocked car parked on the road. Shortly after we passed out in the car, a police officer was knocking on the windows. We got out and the policeman told us to lean over the hood of the car. In my alcohol-fueled and fuzzed mind, I must have decided I needed more rest, because I proceeded to punch the policeman instead. Not one of my more-brilliant moves.

At that point, he got back in his car and called for reinforcements. Another policeman showed up as backup, bringing a very large dog, so I got smart and gave up the fight. I'd already learned that animals can be tough, and I didn't want to go up against a trained police dog. We were taken to jail and charged with car theft because, as luck would have it, someone else had stolen the car and later abandoned it along our stretch of the road. Since we lacked the common sense to not sleep in a stolen car, they assumed we were the ones who'd taken it.

We were jailed (a very sobering experience, literally!) for 14 days before they caught the real car thief. This guy was nabbed in Tennessee for something and confessed to stealing the car. We were released. I never got charged for smacking the policeman, which I would later find out was because they held a lot of respect for the military, and the officer had decided to give me some leeway.

I managed to stay out of trouble for the rest of my time in Hawaii, as well as most of Okinawa, Thailand and Viet Nam, but I sure became good at throwing back those bottles of beer.

In one animal-related incident in Thailand, we were stationed in an old house on top of a mountain near Pak Chong. Here, the top of the mountain was in the clouds most of the time, so visibility was never good. One day, after a few beers, my friend Jake and I went hiking down a mountain trail. I had to stop to pee on a tree, but just as I was doing so we heard a distinct roll of thunder—or so we thought. Instead, it was the growl of a tiger we'd apparently woken up, and he was only a few yards from us!

Not even taking the time to button up (army pants had buttons, not zippers then), Jake and I sobered up real fast, turned tail, and raced back up the mountain trail. When I dared to look back, I saw the tiger was bolting back the other direction. Apparently we'd frightened him just as much as he'd frightened us! I was never so relieved in my life.

On another occasion, I was on guard duty near Lopburi, Thailand. When my shift ended, I walked into town to have a few beers—or a few more than a few. On the way back to camp, I came across a very large python stretched from one side of the road to the other. In my drunken stupor, I couldn't make heads or tails of the situation; in other words, I couldn't tell which end held the mouth and teeth that wanted to eat me! I stood dumbfounded for a few minutes as I tried to reason out how to get around the snake. I still had enough wits about me to know that I didn't want to poke it and piss it off.

Finally, decision made, I walked back a few yards, got a running start, and jumped right over the snake without touching it, continuing to run and looking over my shoulder to make sure he wasn't slithering after me. He wasn't. I was feeling pretty proud of myself that I'd survived an interaction with a python, but when I got back to camp and started bragging about it, I found out the town was off limits to the military. Apparently nobody had thought to tell me this since I was on guard duty, so I landed in a spot of trouble anyway. I lost a stripe, going from an E-3 pay grade back down to an E-2. Even though I hadn't ended up in a snake belly, my day still had a poor ending.

Another time, we had our radio equipment set up in a field of tall grass in Saraburi. One afternoon the power went out, so I was tasked with going outside to change the generators. I had to walk through five-foot high grass to get to the equipment, which was a terrifying prospect in a country with wild creatures readily capable of killing a human. Who knew what could be out there waiting for me in that grass!

Sure enough, as I tentatively stumbled my way out through the weeds, a king cobra suddenly reared up in front of me, looking at me from about a foot above the grass. From my interest in and study of snakes, I knew that king cobras could only get a third of their bodies off the ground. This meant there was still a good 12 more feet of this guy on the ground behind him! No way, he won. I turned around as fast as I could and ran back to the trailer, telling the sergeant we would be down for a while unless he wanted to go out there himself to take care of it. I wasn't going to wrestle with an 18-foot cobra.

In my favorite "bug story" from my time in Thailand, I was riding in the back of a truck, and there was a crane fly buzzing around my head. I thought it was some sort of giant Asian mosquito, and I didn't want to get whatever disease that thing was carrying. So I took a swat at it with a carton of cigarettes, missed, and fell out of the truck, landing on my head in a rice paddy. Turned out I was super lucky, because had I landed on the road instead I would have broken my neck. I would have been the only army casualty killed by a harmless fly.

So much for my early Bugman skills! They, apparently, were nonexistent.

The war had not officially started during my time overseas, but there was a lot of discontent in Viet Nam. I remember seeing one little girl over there who had her hands cut off because she had the audacity to go to school, and that's an image that will stick in my mind until the day I die.

When I was discharged in 1964, I was a full-fledged alcoholic, although I still didn't recognize it. I thought I was just partying and having fun with friends, not realizing the extent to which alcohol had taken over my life. To celebrate my new army-free life, I went to Mexico to party for a bit before heading east to Tiffin, Ohio. The only thing I remember getting out of my visit to Mexico was a horrible case of pubic lice, also known as the crabs. At first I had no idea what had happened to me, but when I finally figured it out, I was in quite a hurry to rid myself of the nasty little buggers.

One person told me the best way to get rid of crab lice is to stab them with an ice pick, which I'm assuming was some kind of joke to see if I'd try it. That seemed a bit much to me and I never got drunk enough to attempt something that drastic. Eventually I used some pesticide I bought in a store and got rid of them that way.

Now, of course, I know non-toxic ways to make them go away, and I'll share these with you later in the book. (The ways to get rid of them, that is—not the crabs. No one wants those!)

I was listless after leaving the military, still not knowing a path for my life or what to do next. I'd developed a friendship with a pen pal named Marlene while I was stationed in Hawaii. Robert Somers, a service friend, lived in Tiffin, Ohio and he had set up the pen pal exchange for me, so I went to visit him and get a chance to spend time with Marlene in person.

When I got to Tiffin, Bob, his wife Joannie, and Marlene met me and we got together, spending much of our time sitting around drinking. I hung out with Marlene for a few months but we weren't romantically compatible, so we ended up going our separate ways. I was working at S.S. Kresge (which later became K-Mart), when I met Barbara Shellhouse and fell in love—we were married on November 26, 1965, when I was 22 years old. Of course, I started my marriage off on the wrong foot because I forgot to go to my own wedding rehearsal—I was out drinking and playing golf with Bob instead. For some fool reason, Barbara married me anyway.

Unbeknownst to my younger self, I would soon have an experience that would shape my future beliefs and actions, even during those days of limited self-awareness.

Barbara's dad, Don, also imbibed and we spent a lot of time together at the local bars. One year Barbara gave me a rifle for Christmas. Since I'd been in the army, I was very familiar with guns and how to operate them. I often went hunting by myself but never killed anything, and I think I was secretly grateful for that. One time I was out, drunk as usual, and I was shooting at birds and missing them all.

I walked back to my car and there happened to be a groundhog sitting nearby. I snuck up from behind and, determined to finally 'get' something, I took aim and shot him/her. Even though I was drunk, this would still be a turning point in my life, because I looked at that groundhog's lifeless body and I just started sobbing. I had no business killing that little animal. I was overcome with remorse for my thoughtless and senseless deed, and there was no way to fix it.

I looked for and found a fork in a tree; I stuck the barrel of the rifle in it and put enough pressure on it to bend the barrel so it would never shoot again. I was only 22, but I was done with hunting. My sense of morality had proven to be stronger than alcohol's effect on my soul.

After my hunting episode, I thought maybe taxidermy would be of more interest to me, so I took a course to see I liked it. The first time I had to skin a dead animal to stuff its body and try to make it look alive, I knew that wasn't the business for me either. There is no doubt in my mind that an animal's skin looks better on the living being than as a decoration on someone's wall.

I also tried horseback riding during that same time period, and it was the first and last time I ever rode a horse. Barbara had this HUGE horse, and she persuaded me to go for a jaunt with her and her friend. So I got in the saddle, but for the life of me couldn't figure out how to make the horse move.

Barbara and her friend went on ahead down the trail, and there I sat, motionless, on the back of a horse who refused to go anywhere. Desperate to not look like the fool I was, I slapped him on the neck and he promptly retaliated by throwing me off into a bunch of bushes.

I decided then and there that if I needed to go anywhere, I'd use a vehicle, not a horse. Turns out I was no cowboy.

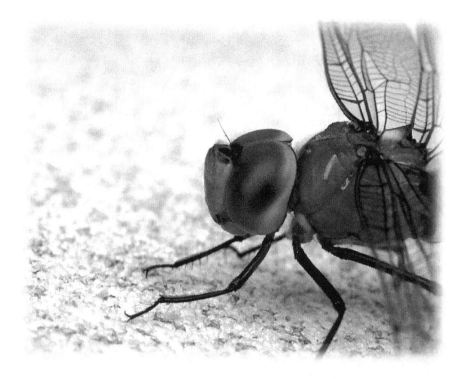

CHAPTER THREE

MY ADVENTURES IN PEST CONTROL BEGIN...
WHILE MY DRINKING WORSENS

We stayed in Ohio through the winter of 1972, Barbara birthing our first son, Rickie, and losing a premature set of twin boys. After so much trauma, we decided to move to Florida where it was warmer and where I would hopefully find better work. I started in the pest control industry, working for

King Pest Control in Hollywood, Florida.

About that time, my drinking took a more serious nose-dive. I even started visiting gay clubs—not because I had any homosexual desires, but I thought maybe it would keep me out of woman-trouble and I could witness a way of life that I'd never seen before. I do remember one time that a fellow came up to me and put his hand on my leg. I stood up, punched him in the nose, and walked out of the bar. I probably was banned after that, as it seems I couldn't even behave myself in a gay bar!

Back to bugs, though. You probably didn't know that I first started in the bug business with a morbid fear of spiders. I don't know if it was "arachnophobia", per se, but I certainly had no wish to be around them. I don't know why I maintained a fear of spiders for so long, but I knew I had to overcome it when I got into pest control.

Arachnophobia comes from the Greek words, "arachne", meaning "spider", and "phobos", meaning "a fear". The fear of spiders may trace its roots to Europe during the Middle Ages. Spiders were considered a source of contamination and any food that came into contact with them was considered poisoned. If they fell into the water it was thought to be undrinkable. Spiders were originally presumed to spread the plague (Black Death) by biting people. Fear of the plague clouded people's perceptions of spiders and they were blamed for all sorts of illnesses and epidemics simply because they were present.

The fear of spiders has persisted in our society for a long time, and this fear is actually encouraged by the pesticide industry. Many companies want to "control" spiders by spraying your home with pesticides, but what they are really doing is preying on your natural fear of the arachnid.

I am not a psychologist and will not try to tell you how to overcome your fear of spiders if you have such a fear. But I will tell you what worked for me. When I got into the bug business, I didn't know a cockroach from a caterpillar, and I was deathly afraid of spiders. The first time I had to crawl under a house I was paralyzed with fear. I decided then and there that if I was going to be successful, I would have to overcome this fear. I started by reading all the literature I could about spiders (much as I'd done for snakes years before), and I watched them spin their webs and stalk their prey. Finally, after several weeks, I let one crawl on me. Oddly enough it didn't bite me and I didn't have a heart attack.

After I overcame that hurdle, I took the next step. I went under houses and crawled through their webs. It was a bit disconcerting at first, but soon I had lost all fear of them. At that point, I decided I needed to get to know them better.

Although most spiders do possess venom glands, most are too small to break the skin with their fangs and have no desire to do so. All spiders will bite in self-defense if they are handled carelessly, such as if they are being squeezed. Most bites occur when people roll over in bed on top of one or the spider is inside their clothing and it bites as it's pressed against the skin.

Don't get me wrong. I'm not saying all spiders are harmless. Black widows are certainly capable of producing a serious bite and any such bite by this spider should be considered a major medical emergency. The brown recluse is also dangerously venomous. Sac spiders and wolf spiders can give serious—though not fatal—bites, particularly if you are allergic to any of the components of the venom.

In my work for King Pest Control, we did monthly pest control by spraying baseboards in people's homes. There were no rules or regulations dealing with applying pesticides in those days. I asked my boss why we sprayed the baseboards and he said it was only to kill time in a customer's house. To make them think they were getting their money's worth.

That was why they sprayed baseboards then, and it's the same reason some companies still spray baseboards today. Let the buyer beware.

Here is how we did a typical cockroach clean-out in those days:

Pest control upkeep was charged at $5 a month. We charged $15 for the initial clean-out, before which the customer was required to empty their kitchen cabinets. Then we went in and sprayed all the cabinets where the food and dishes were kept with chlordane. After that we sprayed all of the baseboards in the house with malathion because it stunk and we wanted the customer to know we weren't using water.

Then we fogged the kitchen with an oil-based pyrethrum using an electric fogging machine. The roaches would come out of the cabinets and get stuck in the oil on the counters. After that we dusted the attic with DDT dust and then put heptachlor granules around the perimeter of the house. We told the people the stuff was safe and they could put their food back in the cabinets when they dried. I no longer believe this was true.

I have no idea how many customers we made sick in those days, but I do know a lot of people who were in the industry that got cancer at an early age. We didn't use any safety equipment, and we drove cars with all the chemicals just sitting in the back seat. And, in those days, I smoked cigarettes, too. I sometimes wonder how I'm still alive!

I remember getting a call about mice infesting a butcher shop in Miami. They sent me down there to take care of the situation. We were told that DDT is a good tracking poison for mice—they walk through it, lick themselves and then die. So when I got to the butcher shop I noticed they had wooden pallets for a floor and the mice were running around under these pallets. The store was open and they had customers in the shop but the owner said to go ahead and treat.

So I got my power duster out of the back seat of my car and proceeded to dust the floor of the store with DDT. The dust was flying everywhere—getting on customers, on the counter, on the meat, everywhere— but I just kept dusting. Finally, the store was full of DDT dust and I was sure all the mice would die.

So I collected my $20 fee and went back to the office. The manager said I did a great job. That's how it was in those days. No one gave a thought to what these poisons were doing to the customers, the environment, the pets, the food. We just went in and waved poison around and hoped it killed what it was supposed to and not what it wasn't supposed to.

One day Barbara and I were sitting in our living room when the phone rang. It was a woman who had a rat in her apartment and wanted to know if I could come right over. I said I could, but I took Barbara with me so she wouldn't think I was going to see a girlfriend. When we got there the woman yelled for us to come in. She was standing on the kitchen table pointing at the bottom of the refrigerator.

Quickly assessing the situation, Barbara realized there really was a rat in there, so she jumped up on the kitchen table with the client. I laid down on my stomach and pointed my flashlight under the refrigerator, not really knowing what else to do. A rat came barreling out, jumped on my shoulder, and ran down my back to the sink cabinet. I almost had a heart attack! So much for being manly. I asked Barbara and the customer to go get some steel wool so I could plug the hole the rat ran into. I plugged the hole and we called it a day. I never heard if the rat came back or not.

Barbara never asked to go on a house call with me again.

Eventually I got promoted to spraying lawns. We used to spray the lawns with dursban, an organophosphate pesticide. We wore shorts and went barefoot. We were told the pesticides were harmless, although now, once again, I'm sure that was far from the truth. I remember one time I was spraying a lawn and when I went around to the backyard, there was an alligator basking in the sun.

I studied my dilemma, which felt strangely like déjà vu from my interactions with the cobra and the python of a few years back. Since I needed to spray the grass, the alligator had to move, so I decided to take action. I got the water hose and gunned it in his direction, which I reasoned would theoretically push him back into the lake. It didn't work. He chased me back to my truck.

The backyard never got sprayed.

Next, I tried my hand in the termite branch. One house we cleaned out had a crawl space, but we couldn't find the entrance and the customer wasn't home. My supervisor said we had to get under that house, so we used our jackhammer and drilled a bunch of holes in a circle in the foundation wall. We then knocked a chunk of cement out and went under the house. Oddly enough we saw daylight coming in from the other side. Apparently nobody had noticed that the entrance to the crawl space was behind a bush. I never found out what the client ever did about the foundation wall we'd destroyed, if anything.

On another occasion, I again had to go into a crawl space to do a termite inspection. The house was near a canal. After I made several turns in the crawl space, my flashlight died and I couldn't see the opening or daylight anywhere. I started crawling toward where I thought the opening was when I heard a low growl. I'd never heard a noise like that and thought there was a dog under the house with me.

Talk about terrifying! I was in the dark with an unknown animal; an animal whose intention seemed to be to attack me if I made a wrong move. Trouble was, I had no idea which way to go or where to turn. I fished out my cigarette lighter (good thing I smoked in those days), lit it, and discovered I'd almost crawled over a six-foot alligator sleeping under the house! Needless to say I dropped my lighter and hightailed it in the opposite direction as fast as I could. It only took a few minutes for me to see the daylight coming through the crawl space opening.

I told the customer I couldn't find any termites, but she had an alligator living under her house. In truth, I didn't know if she had termites or not, as I'd never finished the inspection. She said, oh, yeah, the alligator lived under her house when it wasn't in the canal. She'd just forgotten to tell me about it.

I left King Pest Control because were told that if we read Rachel Carson's book, "Silent Spring", we would be fired. I did, and I was. Rachel's book, which famously documented the effects of pesticides on the environment, springboarded my desire to learn the truth and find environmentally sound ways of pest prevention and removal.

I was now jobless, and so I looked into another industry: professional wrestling. I became a ring announcer for the local wrestling show staged every Friday at the local arena, where I was paid $20 a night plus all the beer I could drink. I'm pretty sure I was getting the better end of that deal.

One night the referee called in sick and the promoter asked me if I would referee the matches. Since all the matches were programmed in advance, I thought it'd be a hoot. All I had to do was look at the timekeeper and he would signal me when the match was supposed to end. I would signal the wrestlers and they would then go into their final hold situation.

Unfortunately, in the last match, one contestant put his opponent in an airplane spin. This was the finishing hold although I wasn't aware of it. I was in the wrong spot in the ring so the spinning wrestler hit me with his feet and knocked me out of the ring, where I landed virtually unconscious. The fellow who was supposed to win was in the ring pinning the villain as scheduled but the referee (me) was laying flat out on the floor.

Fortunately, some wrestlers in the back knew I was in trouble, so they picked me up and threw me back in the ring, where another wrestler jumped in and used my hand to count the bad guy out. The fans loved it and thought it was all part of the show. When I look back on that night now I laugh, but at the time it was pretty painful.

My referee career was over before it even got started, but I did continue as ring announcer for another month or so. I decided I'd better stick with bugs.

It was during that time frame that Barbara's parents came to Florida for a visit, and she decided to move back to Ohio with them shortly after our son Keith was born. I went back a few months later to see if I could be happy living there again, but we were staying with her parents and it was a very difficult situation for everyone. I decided to return to Florida by myself as Barbara wanted no part of it. Our marriage had come to an end.

CHAPTER FOUR

UNTIL YOU HIT ROCK BOTTOM
NOPE, NOT YET

Newly single and still drinking heavily, I got myself involved in some crazy situations, having nothing to do with bugs or pests of any kind. Unless you counted me, I guess.

I was at a bar one night in Ft. Lauderdale when I spotted two attractive women. I went over and hit on the older lady but the younger one, Linda, asked me to dance instead.

Linda was newly divorced, too, and had recently moved to Florida from Alexandria, Virginia. We spent a lot of time

21

together, drinking and partying. We even drove to New York once to visit my sister, and stopped at her home in Alexandria for a brief sojourn. One night she was home and I was getting plastered in a bar in Washington D. C. When I got on the freeway—which is basically a big circle—to go to Alexandria, I couldn't find the exit. So I just drove as fast as I could, hoping I'd just missed it and I'd recognize it on the next pass. Instead, I eventually rear-ended another car, hitting my face on the windshield and falling out of the car onto the highway.

We didn't use seat belts in those days. It turned out I'd fractured my neck, but the police didn't know that and just hauled me off to jail. When I couldn't get up the next day in my cell, they took me to a local hospital where an x-ray showed that my neck was fractured. In a major stroke of luck for me, they dropped the drunk driver charge because the car I hit had been stolen and the thief was in it. I'd inadvertently solved a crime with my drunkenness.

After that experience, I traveled to Houston, Texas and enrolled myself in the Freddie Gage Drug Rehabilitation program, as for the first time it really hit me that I didn't have a handle on my drinking. The program was pretty ridiculous, though, and didn't work for me at all. We would go out at night to bars and stand in front of the doors, telling everyone going in how bad it was and trying to stop them. The whole time I was supposed to be talking folks out of going inside, I just wanted to be the one going in myself, and not the idiot standing outside feeling the fool. So I left the program.

I next decided to visit California, so I hopped on a bus and spent a week or so in San Francisco where I met a young lady of "ill repute". She was young and forced to do what she did to make a living, since she had run away from her home in San Diego and had no skills or money to survive on. She was desperate for a way out, and I decided I would help her.

I got us a couple of bus tickets to San Diego, went back to her apartment one night when her pimp was out, and spirited her away. I got to see her go home and make up with her folks, and for once I felt like I'd actually done some good in the world.

Yet I continued drinking, somehow still functioning in my day to day life. I returned to Houston where I moved to a little apartment and got a job as a salesman for Truly Nolan Pest Control. When the manager moved on, the district manager offered me the job as branch manager of the office. Of course I said "YES!" and loved the sales meetings and flying to other areas, always making sure to get my free drinks on the expense account.

One time when I was the manager of the Truly Nolen branch in Houston I couldn't find one of our route-men. We didn't have cell phones in those days but they were supposed to check in periodically from one of those antiquated phone booths.

I drove his route area and saw his truck parked next to a pasture. He wasn't in the truck, but when I looked out into the pasture, there he was turning over cow pies looking for psychedelic mushrooms. He found plenty, too. Apparently he did this quite often. Not knowing what to say, I told him not to use the mushrooms while at work and he assured me he wouldn't. He said he smoked a lot of pot though, as it was easier to spray a house if he was totally stoned. He didn't get a raise that year, but I didn't fire him either.

I went to a restaurant in Missouri City one night that was being treated for German cockroaches. The two servicemen should have been finished with the job much earlier but were still there. I went in to see what the holdup was, and noticed they were acting oddly. I walked over and they were each spraying small circles around individual cockroaches, basically killing the roaches in the restaurant one at a time! It turns out they smoked "a little" pot before going to work that night. They were so messed up I had to call a couple of other fellows to come finish the job properly and get these guys home.

One of the most embarrassing situations I ever had to deal with in the pest control industry took place in Houston during my time with Truly Nolen. I got a call about lice or something, they weren't sure what the problem was. When I got to the house, the lady of the house let me in and told me she was being bitten by "something". She wanted me to identify the pest and treat for it. I said OK.

I should have suspected something was amiss because her husband was sitting on the couch smoking a joint, ignoring everything that was going on around him. When I introduced myself, it was evident he was totally stoned.

The young lady asked me to look through her hair for lice. Feeling a bit uncomfortable, I ran my fingers through her hair with one hand while shining a flashlight on her head with the other. It was a little nerve wracking, especially since I couldn't find anything. She then stepped back and dropped her shorts (no underwear), and asked me to examine her pubic area for bugs, as she was also itching in that area. Feeling very foolish, I dropped to my knees and focused my flashlight on her pubic area, trying to figure out how to move the hair around without actually touching her.

Finally, I pulled a pen out of my pocket and started searching through her pubic hair using the pen cap to part the hair. After what seemed like hours, but was probably only two minutes, I stood up and said I didn't see any bugs. I was totally mortified and red-faced, and turned around quickly so she could redress without me watching—which was probably ridiculous considering what had just occurred.

Her husband was on the couch laughing himself silly because of my obvious embarrassment. I didn't treat for anything even though they wanted me to spray their whole house; I just wanted to get out of there as fast as I could. I'm not a prude by any stretch of the imagination, but I was totally unprepared for that service call and didn't know how to react. To this day I'm not sure if they were trying for a sexual encounter or if they were so high they believed they were covered in bugs.

One day I was driving a new Truly Nolen truck to the office when someone ran a stop sign and broadsided me. The truck rolled over several times and burst into flames, but not before I flew out through the windshield and landed on someone's lawn. I was lucky we didn't wear seatbelts at the time...had I had a seat belt on, I would have been toast—literally.

I did seriously injure my shoulder, and the doctors at the emergency room thought I pulled all the tendons out of my shoulder and would never be able to use my right arm again. I thought I would be handicapped for life, so I was sitting in a bar one day drinking beer with my left arm and generally being depressed. For some reason, without thinking, I reached for the bottle of beer on the bar with my right arm, grabbed it, and took a drink.

The person next to me reminded me that my right arm didn't work—but all of a sudden it had, and it DID! I was elated. I headed for the driving range to see if I could hit a golf ball and, by gum, I could. The arm still worked. I don't know how or why, but I was healed!

The doctors had no idea how that could have possibly happened, but I suspect a Higher Power, even in those days, was looking after me.

CHAPTER FIVE

REMARRIED...AND THEN, FINALLY, ROCK BOTTOM?

After I got my right arm back, I felt like I had a new lease on life, and the stretch continued when I met the beautiful Sandi Widner in Albuquerque.

The Truly Nolen branch manager in Albuquerque needed a mouse car, which is a yellow Volkswagon tricked out with ears and a tail so that it looked like a mouse. I drove the mouse car to Albuquerque from Houston, and Sandi was there that day, working in the Albuquerque office. Sandi and I hit if off immediately, making me a believer in love at first sight. We went to dinner and walked along the river, and by the end of the night, I was hooked.

When I got back to Houston, just that fast, I called her and proposed to her. She must have felt the same way, because she said "YES!", then flew out to Houston with her son Bodie. The Albuquerque manager was livid that I was going to steal and marry his secretary and he complained to the district manager, who just laughed it off.

Sandi and I were married on July 9th, 1976 in Missouri City, Texas, where we said our "I Do's" in front of a Justice of the Peace and two gay fellows, who served as best man and maid of honor. A bunch of bikers threw rice on us as we left the building. It was a memorable day.

Our son Bryan was born in Houston on April 23rd of the next year. He came so quickly that his head was crowning before I even could get parked in front of the emergency entrance. The emergency staff ran out to get Sandi, and she delivered him before I could get into the building. Apparently Sandi didn't believe in long labor.

Sandi shared my love of snakes, so we always kept a few snakes as companions. One afternoon I was sitting on the couch reading the paper while Sandi was handling a small garter snake. The doorbell rang. Sandi went to get the door because she was expecting someone, and she put the snake inside her blouse to scare them. She wasn't wearing a bra.

When she opened the door, the movement of her arm must have startled the snake, because it bit her and attached itself to her nipple. She screamed, ripped off her shirt, and was jumping up and down with the snake hanging from her breast. The folks at the door were not the guests she was expecting, but instead two Jehovah's Witnesses. Can you imagine their surprise? Their jaws dropped, their eyes became as big as saucers and they screamed, ditching their literature and running down the sidewalk yelling "Devil woman, devil woman". I never laughed so hard in my life.

In fact, it took me a few minutes to calm myself enough so I could disconnect the snake from Sandi's nipple. Sandi was understandably quite traumatized herself at first, but she soon saw the humor in the situation, and it became one of our favorite stories.

In 1977 we moved to San Antonio, where I worked for Orkin Pest Control as route-man in the hill country of Texas. During our time there, Sandi adopted a doberman who was freed from a dog-fighting group, and we fostered some Great Dane puppies she rescued, too. The dobie passed away from old age in a short amount of time, but the puppies grew strong and we adopted some of them out into good homes.

We drove to Florida that year to spend Thanksgiving with my family, and I was blessed to see my mom and dad for the last time. Dad was very sick, and he apologized to me for not adopting me legally when I was young. I told him not to worry about it and that I would just adopt him instead. A couple of years later I legally changed my last name from Mosher to Fagerlund and "adopted" my step-father.

Sandi and I moved around a lot in those years, perhaps trying to keep our marriage intact, but it just didn't work out. Sandi also used to indulge in drinking almost as much as I did, and we would end up getting in some pretty heated arguments while under the influence of alcohol.

We had a daughter, Sara, who was born on April 7, 1979. Sandi and split up shortly after and went our separate ways. Although Sandi and I got a divorce in 1980 we ended up remaining very good friends.

When we first moved back to Albuquerque, I worked for a couple pest control companies, but things usually went south, so I decided to try my luck at my own business. Apparently it didn't work out very well either, because I can't even remember what I'd named my company! Alcohol definitely had me in its clutches by this point, and my life was spiraling ever downward. I was just too high and stubborn to see it.

I remember one incident that happened during that chaotic period in my life. I was under a house looking for termites when I crawled over a black widow spider. Since I was only wearing a t-shirt, the spider managed to bite me on an exposed part of my stomach. I understood that the spider was acting in self-defense because I was squishing it. He hadn't come after me, I had attacked him, from his perspective. I calmly got out of the crawl space and drove back to Albuquerque, where I told Sandi what had happened. She asked me if I wanted to go to the hospital, but I said no…so I just sat in an easy chair for a few days and she fed me plenty of beer and food and eventually the bite symptoms went away. For the first couple of days it felt like I had a charlie-horse in every muscle in my body. That was probably not the smartest decision I'd ever made, but it's what I did, and I lived to tell the tale.

I eventually went to work for Orkin again, where I was in sales and did fairly well. I would drive up to Santa Fe and knock on doors for commercial accounts, bringing in business for the company and making a decent living for myself.

But I continued drinking, driving, getting in fights in bars, and sleeping with women whose names I never even knew—and God only knows what else. I often wonder how I survived that time in my life. I met a guy named Cal who also liked snakes, so we went looking for snakes frequently while we drank a lot of beer. One time down in the Magdalena Mountains we came upon some rock rattlesnakes nesting behind a group of boulders. One small snake took off, so I grabbed it by its tail. Duh! Of course it turned around and bit me.

I drank a few beers but decided that wasn't going to work because the bite was too painful. Cal took me to the Socorro hospital, but they didn't know what to do for snakebite so they had me transported to a hospital in Albuquerque. I spent several days there with tubing in both arms. My blood pressure wasn't stable and they were afraid I was dehydrating. I told them to give me a couple of beers and I would be fine. They opted instead for a catheter, which was much more painful than the snakebite.

Finally I begged them to take it out the next morning and I promptly checked out of the hospital after signing a waiver. I drove down to Magdalena the next weekend to catch another rock rattlesnake. I had to prove to myself that I wasn't afraid of them. I was able to catch one, and satisfied myself the fear hadn't taken hold.

Another time I was feeding a copperhead I cared for in my home collection, and he bit me. I decided the best medicine was a fifth of scotch, which I drank and then promptly passed out. The next morning the whole left side of my body was swollen, so back to the hospital I went, again. In a four-year period I was bitten nine times by venomous snakes, mostly rattlesnakes. I have never been bitten sober.

Statistics actually state that most snakebite victims are young white males under the influence of alcohol. I fit that criteria every time. Most people I tell would mention that the word "dumb" should be added in there, too. Yeah, maybe.

I was still bouncing around from pest control company to pest control company, not able to find a good fit and amazed at the incompetence of most of the companies. I imagine my drinking affected my work and ability to evaluate my situation to the best of my ability, but at the time I certainly didn't see that as a problem.

Until the day I finally hit bottom.

On December 23rd, 1985, Sandi and Bryan and I were sitting in a bar in Albuquerque. We were arguing about something stupid and yelling at each other. The bartender came over and told us to calm down, so I proceeded to throw a pitcher of beer at him. Next the bouncer came over, and I somehow had the strength to knock him out. I then got in my car, drove home, and passed out.

The next morning was Christmas Eve, and I awoke with the worst hangover I'd ever experienced in my life . . . and I've had my fair share. I swore I would never take another drink of alcohol in my life, and—believe it or not—I've kept that promise.

I was done.

Two weeks later, I also quit smoking cigarettes, and I was a three-pack-a-day smoker. I never went to a meeting or took anything to aid me in these endeavors. I simply made a decision, and after that it was all sheer willpower (with the help of God).

Sandi and I got along better after we were divorced than while we were married. Sadly though, Sandi was killed in a car accident in Roswell, New Mexico, in March of 1991. I will never forget the moment I found out, how bereft I felt when Anna called me at 4 a.m. in the morning to let me know what had happened. I went to Roswell to her funeral, and it was an incredibly sad occasion. Sandi was a beautiful person, and I still love her to this day. I really wish we could have had an alcohol-free marriage—we'd probably still be together if we had.

Sandi, as I will always remember her.

Having had many years to think about alcohol—not just my relationship to it, but the fact that so many struggle with this particular demon—I believe that the problem with alcohol is that it is just too readily available. Our governments, federal and local, keep trying to restrict the use of marijuana, which is almost harmless compared to booze, but they don't do anything to confront the real problem.

In New Mexico we have a very high rate of driving under the influence arrests and yet these same people are re-arrested time and again for the same crime. We put people in the penitentiary for many years for marijuana possession, but let drunk drivers continue to wreak havoc on the highways.

Proponents of alcohol will say we tried prohibition and it didn't work. But maybe we need to revisit how alcohol is consumed. My suggestion would be prohibiting the sale of alcohol either in retail or in bars or lounges after 7 p.m. I would also require all bars to limit all customers to three drinks maximum. If they are caught selling a fourth drink, shut the establishment down for 30 days.

All of the bars would get the hint sooner or later. If people want to drink at night, let them drink at home, that way they won't have to drive drunk. If someone has a party at night and some folks get drunk, then the party-giver is responsible for setting them up for the night.

Drinking socially is fine, but almost all of the drunks that drive are either leaving bars after having consumed large quantities of alcohol or leaving a party after consuming a lot of booze. You very rarely see anyone pulled over for driving under the influence of marijuana.

Time to refocus our priorities.

CHAPTER SIX

THE UNIVERSITY OF NEW MEXICO...AND BEYOND

After leaving alcohol behind, I gradually got my life in order, and increased my ability to make wiser decisions for myself and my future. I realized that I genuinely had a passion for learning all I could about environmentally-safe pest control, and a desire to protect both bugs and humans from destructive practices. Finally, in 1995, I gave up working for pest control companies and went to work for the University of New Mexico as their pest control specialist. I spent 11 years with UNM before retiring, and it was there that I got the opportunities to really make a difference in the way they, and people all across the country, looked at pest prevention.

While they promoted the least-toxic pest management style available, they still wanted to use anything they could on the premises to get quick results—and that usually included toxic pesticides. Eventually I insisted on using the least-toxic products, and the campus community got behind it and loved it.

One time some folks killed an antelope on the Sevilleta National Wildlife Refuge, which was managed by UNM, and I contacted Senator Pete Domenici to get his help to make the refuge safer for animals. He contacted UNM and made a lot of noise, which of course they weren't happy about. My boss, Mary, asked me if I called Senator Domenici and I said "no." She smiled. Then I said "I emailed him." She didn't smile. She was furious, and didn't want me contacting senators or anyone else about UNM business. No whistle-blowing is what she meant—but of course it's illegal for her to tell me I can't whistleblow. So I kept doing it, and she kept not liking it.

I started writing columns about pest control when I was with the university, and loved every minute of it. I wrote frequent bug articles for the UNM Daily Lobo and then started writing for the Albuquerque Tribune in 1996. Soon my columns appeared in all of the Scripps-Howard papers, which was the parent company of the Tribune. I quit the Tribune in 2001 and went to the Albuquerque Journal, instead, and in doing so lost most of the Scripps papers. I also wrote for the Santa Fe New Mexican, the Socorro E Defense Chieftain, the Valencia County New-Bulletin, and Prime Time.

I still enjoy writing columns for various papers, because I like helping people solve their pest problems without having to use toxic pesticides. I have received hundreds if not thousands of letters from readers around the country. Here is a sample of the comments and letters I've received:

Hello, Richard,

Just a quick and strong thank you for all the times you have written to debunk the California Department of Agriculture's witless and fanatic passion for trying to spray us all with poisons. I have kids and grandkids and some of us have asthma. We live in Alameda County, which was to be next on their spray schedule. I am so glad we have managed to get the spraying postponed, and I think a lot of the credit goes to you. (And I think your column is great in general, too.) Bravo, and carry on!"

"Your articles in the San Francisco Chronicle are a must-read for anyone with any brain in their head. I especially like your respect for the diverse web of life. AND you once owned and actually liked a rat. That is way cool. 'One has not known true love until one has loved a rat.'—Carl Jung. Mine was named Ratsky.

Of course I got negative letters, too, which is the way of the world. Some people love you while others hate you and what you're doing, even when you believe you are making the world a better place. Here's one I got from someone in the pest control industry, who was annoyed that I was "picking on" the industry. They thought I was over-reacting to the dangers of pesticides:

I don't know you, but I read a story about kids and pesticides. Some of the information was good, however I think you have exaggerated some of your writing. Being in the pest control industry for almost as long as you (1975) I take great offense to people that write stories to get people scared about what we really do. Yes, I do agree that children in a group environment such as daycare, school, and others should not be in the same area when an application is being made. But if the kids are inside and the service is outside, then where is the harm? Most of the new products we use have been engineered to work on specific aspects only the Arthropod class of animals have. Please try not to exaggerate the bad points about pest control. The good points, benefits, greatly outweigh the hazards."—Steve S.

He asked, where is the harm if children are inside and the service is done outside? Here's just one example in terms of rebuttal: On Oct. 11, 2011, a pest control person was applying a herbicide on school property in Ohio. The herbicide contained 2-4-D. Forty-seven children inside that school were poisoned by the spray and six had to be hospitalized. Where is the harm, he says? I believe that's obvious, and this is why I wrote and still write columns today.

In 1998 I met Johnna Lachnit (now Johnna Lynn Dewberry) on campus. She would turn out to be absolutely instrumental in my life, and even co-authored the below books with me. I met Johnna when she asked me for help with an article on pesticides for a publication she was producing. Our working relationship grew from there, as Johnna is an expert with computers, and I was considered the expert in all things bug, so we ended up developing future projects together.

I wrote two books while working for UNM, both published by UNM Press. The first was entitled "Ask the Bugman", and was based on my columns and published in 2002. The second book, "The Bugman on Bugs", was published in 2004, and was also co-authored by Johnna.

Former governor of New Mexico Gary Johnson wrote the foreword for "The Bugman on Bugs", and now that he's actually run for president, that makes it all the more fun. Gary wrote:

> "Richard Fagerlund and Johnna Strange have once again delivered a book that is equally entertaining and informative. In this book, Mr. Fagerlund discusses the various types of common pests and the ways they are most typically exterminated.
>
> However, the problem, according to the "Bugman," is not the pest itself, but the pesticides used to exterminate them. Common pesticides have been proven extremely harmful, if not fatal, to animals and also humans. There must be a stop to the unnecessary use of these dangerous chemicals.
>
> Alternatives must also be given for what we use pesticides on. Cotton, for example, attracts nine different kinds of pests; as a result, twenty-nine different pesticides are sprayed. Cotton's alternative, hemp, only attracts two pests, whose removal does not require a pesticide. Hemp, if decriminalized, can help reduce the amount of pesticides deposited into the air, providing a safer environment for both humans and animals.
>
> By eliminating frequent misconceptions and replacing them with facts, Richard Fagerlund and Johnna Strange lead the way to a better, healthier planet, where pollution from pesticides is limited."

After I left the University of New Mexico, Johnna and I wrote a third book with two other authors (that was never conventionally published), entitled "What are we Doing, Our

Children are Watching". The Foreword to this book was written by the President of the Humane Society of the United States, Wayne Pacelle. Wayne said in the forward:

"In this work, Dick Fagerlund and his co-authors Holly Fagerlund, Johnna Strange, and Viki Elkey bring both intelligence and wit to bear on some rather grim and decidedly humorless pursuits like dog fighting, cockfighting, hog-dog fights, and rattlesnake roundups. I commend it to anyone who wants to learn more about the bad things that can happen to animals when those of us who know better fail to stand up to those who do not. I especially commend it to anyone who may be under the impression that such activities and spectacles are clean, innocent fun, in which no one is harmed. Drawing on personal communication and experience with the enthusiasts and defenders of animal fighting, in a state (New Mexico) where the battle has lately been joined, Fagerlund et al let the perpetrators indict themselves. And indict themselves they do. As serious as these matters are, I couldn't help but find amusement in the shoddy reasoning of these individuals, tradition bearers for activities that are already illegal in the majority of states. Still, this is a serious work, one that calls upon us all to do what we can, through legislation, education, and public awareness, to put these unworthy pursuits behind us."

During my time with UNM, I co-wrote three scientific papers on bugs; this isn't something I'd continue to do in the future, as the writing is boring and laborious, and very few people actually read the finished product—usually just scholarly folks with interest in the insects you've written about.

That being said, below are listings of the three papers, two with co-authors on campus and one with an entomologist from the University of Texas, El Paso. The last one about fleas and lice lists me as the second author, but I actually conceived the paper and wrote most of it. Since it was published by a government agency and one of their folks, Paulette Ford, was a co-author, they listed her as senior author.

Mackay, W. P., and R. Fagerlund. 1997.
"Range expansion of the red imported fire ant, *Solenopsis invicta* Buren (Hymenoptera: Formicidae), into New Mexico and extreme West Texas." Proceedings of the Entomological Society of Washington 99:758-759.

Fagerlund, R.; Ford, P. L.; Brown, T.; Polechla, P. J., Jr. 2001.
New records for fleas (Siphonaptera) from New Mexico with notes on plague-carrying species. Southwestern Naturalist. 46: 94-95.

Ford, Paulette L.; Fagerlund, Richard A.; Duszynski, Donald W.; Polechla, Paul J. 2004.
Fleas and lice of mammals in New Mexico. Gen. Tech. Rep. RMRS-GTR-123. Fort Collins, CO: U.S. Department of Agriculture, Forest Service, Rocky Mountain Research Station. 57 p.

I specialized in flies during my tenure as an entomologist at UNM. I was listed as a Dipterist (specialist in flies) in North America, and still am:

Richard Fagerlund, Environmental Services, University of New Mexico, Albuquerque, NM 87131, USA. Telephone: (505)

277-9904. Fax: (505) 277-1250. E-mail: fagerlun@unm.edu
Interests: Dipteran biodiversity in New Mexico, particularly
cecidomyiids, agromyzids and tephritids.

Now I am years retired from the field, and no longer practice any entomology outside of pest management, but I am still
considered a "Dipterist".

One of my most-interesting experiences at UNM came
around 1996. I was collecting insects in the Gila Wilderness
in southwest New Mexico when I found several salamanders
that I knew immediately were an undescribed species. As
mentioned earlier, I have a background in herpetology before
I went into entomology, so I was fairly certain I was correct. I
captured four adults and brought them home with me, asking
the herp fellow at the college what I should do next.

He said they would examine them, preserve them, (i.e. kill
them) and then go down and find more, to see how far they
ranged. I thought about that for awhile and then decided there
was no reason to do all of that. I brought the salamanders
(a five hour drive) back to where I found them and released
them. I have been back twice in the last fifteen years and they
are still there and they seem very pleased that nobody knows
they exist.

At least nobody has trampled all over their habitat looking for them. The herp guy was annoyed, of course, as he was
looking forward to publishing a paper on a new species of
salamander. Personally, I believed the salamanders were better
off remaining anonymous.

The question for me becomes, is it necessary to go out and
kill a lot of insects or other small animals while documenting
a new species if they have absolutely no impact on humans,
economically or in any other way? I don't believe it is.

I did a lot of arthropod identifications over the years for

government agencies such as the Bandelier National Monument, Jornada, and others. I was well-paid—with taxpayer money—to identify these arthropods, but we frequently found rodents, shrews, lizards and salamanders dead in the pitfall traps.

It left a bad taste in my mouth. Did we have to execute all of these animals just to determine what kind of arthropods are living in a mountain, desert or riparian habitat? Should these kinds of studies that have absolutely no economical meaning be funded by taxpayer dollars? At the time I didn't make a big stink about it, but the more I think about it, the more I disagree with it.

Maybe all of these arthropods and other animals that will never react with humans would be much better off if we left them alone. We can put the money toward entomological pursuits such as household pests, lawn and ornamental pests, disease vectors, and arthropods that actually interact with us in some way. This goes for other groups of animals as well.

We don't really need to know what kind of animals live at the bottom of the ocean, do we? Someone mentioned we could probably put the salamanders on the Endangered Species List (ESL) since they are so limited in distribution. In checking into this, I discovered that, as of this writing, there are currently 714 species of insects and other arthropods on the Endangered Species List. If that number isn't high enough, there are 944 species of snails on the ESL, 105 species of clams, 17 species of worms, and 1 centipede on the ESL. There are undoubtedly thousands more that have become extinct without ever having been "discovered" by humans.

One doesn't always know what the best answer is, but I know that both the salamanders and I remain happier that they are "free", and that's good enough for me.

I had the opportunity to teach a couple of classes in entomology in the biology department while I was with UNM, even though I had never attended college myself. I was listed as a Board Certified Entomologist—designated by the Entomological Society of America (ESA)—because I took a test proving I knew what I was talking about. One doesn't necessarily need a college degree to become learned in his/her chosen area of interest and passion.

So I taught two semesters with Sandy Brantley as my co-instructor, and we had a success on our hands. I wish we could have gotten to do more teaching, because I really enjoyed it. We asked the students to write critiques of the class and every single student gave it and our instruction a positive review.

When I joined the ESA, I needed a reference from another entomologist, and Dr. Jenella Loye of the Dept. of Entomology at University of California Davis wrote the following letter to the Entomological Society of America on my behalf:

"To Whom it May Concern:

It is with great pleasure that I recommend for membership Mr. Richard Fagerlund. Dick Fagerlund is a highly competent ecologist for insects and other arthropods in New Mexico. In addition he has worldwide interests and works with the Museum of the Department of Zoology at the University of New Mexico to identify and catalogue a diversity of species from international study sites.

Dick is a tireless proponent of the field of Entomology. He teaches at the University where he also directs the integrated pest management for the campus. I have never seen such dedication to community outreach. Dick writes a column for the Albuquerque Journal, directs non-profit training programs for the pest control industry, publishes

*a monthly Pest Control Operator newsletter (also distrib-
uted free) and advises the entire community in Northern
New Mexico on pest problems whenever they call. He is
an amazingly productive entomologist and epitomizes the
traditions that brought me to entomology and have kept
me in the field – that of curiosity, enthusiasm and support
for those with interest and need to learn.*

*We are so lucky to have Dick Fagerlund join the E.S.A.
I look forward to a chance to see him active at meetings.
We certainly need him on our team."*

I remember one last UNM incident that happened shortly
before I retired. I was called to rescue a squirrel that was caught
in a pipe. It appeared that the helpless little guy had been in the
pipe for several days, and was seriously dehydrated. I pulled
him out and he was breathing, but barely. I put a little water
on his lips and he moved. I put the little angel in a box on a
towel and took him home to Holly. We tried for several hours
to revive the squirrel, but to no avail. He was ready to move on
and explore another universe.

From the time I pulled him from the pipe, to when I introduced him to Holly, to when he passed on, we never stopped
thinking about how to save him. It didn't help; Rocky's time
was at an end. I have no idea why a single squirrel out of
hundreds of animals, birds, and lower forms of life that I met
every day would stick out so much in my thoughts and totally
consume my time. But he did.

Isn't every squirrel the same? What is the difference
between Rocky and the squirrel you see on the road that got
hit by a car? Holly and I had been afforded the gift and the
opportunity to look into Rocky's eyes, even as they were only
half-open. We saw his little heart and glowing soul, and we

caressed him, hoping to revive his will to live.

We don't know why he left, but we do know we saw a little smile in his eyes when we looked at him. We both shed a few tears over a squirrel we'd only known for a few hours, but who epitomized the life and loves of every squirrel—no, every animal—we have ever met or will meet in the future.

Someone once said that when a butterfly dies in the jungle, the whole world changes. I don't know for sure, but maybe there is some truth to that. I can say that when a little soul went to the next plateau in our living room, our world changed, and it changed for the better, becoming deeper and enriched.

It boggles the mind to think that there are people on this planet who go out and shoot, or—worse yet—trap any living thing and deliberately destroy its heart and soul. Every animal, every being in the universe shares the single soul of the Creator, and I hope that if you look into the eyes of any animal this will become as clear to you as it is to me.

We looked into Rocky's eyes while he was with us, and we saw his little soul and we loved what we saw. Rocky passed through our hearts and Holly and I are richer for it.

CHAPTER SEVEN

HOLLY AND I DABBLE IN ANIMAL RESCUE

I met Holly Kern online at a cockfighter's discussion board in 2003. We both used to get on there to watch these idiots talk about cockfighting, and we wanted to put a stop to it. (More on cockfighting later.) Holly was separating from her husband in Louisiana, so she came out to Albuquerque to get some distance from the situation, but she ended up staying a while longer as we were married on June 5th, 2005.

Holly and I got involved in animal rescue quite accidentally. Our first rescue dog was an Australian shepherd that we adopted during a seminar in Corrales. We named her Sacajawea (Wea). We leased a farm with a barn, corral, and a couple of sheds in Moriarty, and moved there with Sacajawea and Chepi, another Australian shepherd we adopted, and Flash, a Dalmatian cross. Chepi was found wandering the streets near Gallup, New Mexico, covered with ticks.

We also brought with us Dakota, a Dalmatian we had flown in from Arizona where he was going to be put down, and Tuki, a blind Dachshund who was dumped in the desert.

Shortly after we moved in, two Akitas found their way into the yard. They had tags so we called their owner, who said she would come and get them as they liked to wander. A few days later she called us and said her husband wouldn't let her have the dogs back. We told the Akitas, who we named Ralphie and Buttercup, that we would feed them while we searched for adopters if they hung around and watched the place; that seemed to be agreeable to them, too.

In fact, they were such good watchdogs that one night, Ralphie, Buttercup and a goat named Fifi actually chased a mountain lion out of the yard.

A week or so later, Holly went to the gate where Ralphie and Buttercup were barking. She found a dog hiding in a bush with a six-week old puppy, who was crying. The adult dog was totally blind and the puppy was deaf. They were catahoulas, a breed that some soulless humans use in hog/dog rodeos (hog butchery).

We had our hands full.

Then someone asked Holly if she would take a box of puppies that were only two weeks old, and needed to be bottle-fed. Holly told the person we didn't have any more room, but when Holly went back into the house, they left the box of puppies by the gate anyway.

Freddie, a German shepherd, wandered in the yard after being scalded with boiling water and burnt with cigarettes. He was so scared when I first met him that he would roll over on his back and start urinating, trembling in fear. After a couple of months, Freddie got past much of his trauma, became a more-confident dog, and we were able to find him a good home.

Holly also loved snakes and she would frequently pick them up and relocate them so they wouldn't get hurt. Not the venomous ones, though—she called me in for those.

One day she called me as I was pulling into the driveway, panicking because there was a rattlesnake in the shed and our Dalmatian, Dakota, was going after it. I went straight to the shed and there was a good-sized prairie rattlesnake rattling his tail off, really frightened and dangerous in that state. Holly held Dakota back, and I picked up the snake and took it to the far end of the property to release it.

When we lived in Veguita, there were always dozens of rattlesnakes on the property at all times. I was constantly relocating them. Our dogs did get bit a few times, but every one of them survived the bite. One really honest vet told us all we had to do is give the dog a Benadryl, and they would most-likely be fine. He believed all the snake-bite vaccinations were worthless. We took his advice and when a dog got bit, he or she got a Benadryl and we never lost a dog from it. I love honest veterinarians.

Another day Holly found a Great Pyrenees puppy tied to our gate. It was obvious he was beaten, as he was very scared and cried incessantly. It took several weeks of tender loving care for Harry to come around. He became a gentle giant who loved to play and was very emotionally mature; it's a shame he had to be mistreated to find his way into a better situation.

At one point a car drove by and threw out what we thought was a black bag of trash. It turned out to be a black Scottish terrier, instead. The dog was not hurt physically that we could see, but emotionally he was a mess. It took several days for him to calm down; once he learned to trust again he began eating properly and quickly recovered.

One day Holly found a six-foot python crawling through our yard, after he had apparently been dumped off nearby. We took "Monty" in and kept him for a year or so and he did very well, but I finally decided he needed to be in a larger reptile environment, so I transferred him to the Rattlesnake Museum in Albuquerque. Last I heard, Monty was still going strong.

Holly and I ended up getting a divorce, and our adventures in the world of animal rescue came to an end. We placed many animals into loving homes during our time together, though, and so for that aspect alone our adventure still holds meaning for both of us today; we remain friends.

When I retired from the University of New Mexico in 2006, I went into pest management consulting. I still help people and businesses control pests using least-toxic methods—promoting this in my columns, on Facebook, Twitter, and anywhere else that I can.

I will pick up and drive anywhere in New Mexico to help someone if I have to.

I also work with pest management companies that I consider honest and competent to solve some of their pest problems using least-toxic methods. I will refer business to any company that meets my standards of honesty and competency, but not many do.

Today I live more of a quiet, retired life; I spend time with my family, and keep up to date all I can with recent discoveries and science regarding bugs, snakes, and all the creatures that many other folks would describe as creepy.

I can honestly say most have never been creepy to me.

CHAPTER EIGHT

MY PHILOSOPHY ON THE USE AND
ABUSE OF ANIMALS IN OUR SOCIETY

As we come to the end of my personal reflections on my own history, laughter, and struggles along my path to The Bugman, I'd like to end this front section of the book with a brief glimpse into my beliefs on the use and abuse of animals in our society.

After all these years and everything that I have experienced, I can't really complain about the state of my health. For my age and all the abuse I've put my body through, I'm actually in surprisingly good condition. Every time I take a physical my lab work comes back normal, which is surprising after all of the pesticides I have been around and my over-indulgence of alcohol and tobacco in my early to mid-years.

I can see the pesticide industry now using this to point out how safe their chemical are. "Look at The Bugman, he used pesticides all the time and he is perfectly healthy!" I actually had one pest control person say this exact thing to me. In reality, I believe that I am relatively healthy because in my childhood we ate meat, but it was organic, from a small farmer. The chicken, beef, or pork wasn't loaded down with chemicals, hence my immune system got off to a positive start. I am now vegan, and don't consume any meat or animal products at all, and I feel all the more healthy for it.

People much younger than me have eaten most of their foods from factory farms where all of the meat is contaminated with all sorts of chemicals and pesticides. Children eating this stuff have a compromised immune system and are more likely to get sick earlier in life. That is why I recommend that nobody eats any meat that you buy at a supermarket or a Walmart, as they are not in any way organic. If you have to eat meat—and you don't—try to get some from a local rancher if you have one around. Or, at least, eat only food that is labeled "certified organic."

Do animals have souls? I don't doubt it for a minute. How can you look into the eyes of a puppy and not see a soul? How can you watch kittens cavort playfully for hours and not accept the fact that they are enjoying life as only God can give it?

Conversely, when you are walking in the wilderness and

you hear the scream of an animal in unbearable pain, how could you not believe that animal shares the same love from God as the puppy and the kittens? That animal, whether it is a coyote, a skunk, a raccoon, a bear cub, or a bobcat kitten, could be screaming because he/she stepped into one of man's vilest inventions—the leghold trap. If this is the case and the animal is "lucky", someone will come along and put them out of their misery. More likely, though, the trap will hold these poor beings indefinitely until they are either dead or chew their own leg off to escape, suffering by themselves in the wilderness, interminably crippled and resigned to a certain, slow death.

What gives mankind the right to savagely end the life and destroy the soul of innocent creatures? Who came to the conclusion that some mindless twit would look better dressed in the bloody skin of a harmless animal than allowing that animal to live out his/her life as God intended? What segment of our society not only endorses such behavior but also believes it is justifiable?

When you think of evil, you probably think of people like Adolf Hitler, Pot Pol, Idi Amin, Joseph Stalin, and other genocidal maniacs. When you think of terrorists, you think of Neo-Nazis, the Aryan Nation, Al-Qaeda, etc. But, in my opinion, no list of terrorists should be complete without including cockfighters, dogfighters, trappers, trophy hunters, and others who abuse animals.

Terrorism, whether perpetrated against humans or animals, is still terrorism. We all share the love and soul of the divine and any form of torture to anyone or anything else is terrorism in its cruelest form.

What can we do to change society so we all can respect each other and treat each other as we should? I believe it is crucial that we legally do away with all forms of cruelty, whether it is against humans or animals. We have to teach our children that abuse against animals of any species is just wrong.

We have to teach our children that circuses without animals are better than circuses where they beat the animals so they will do stupid tricks for human amusement. We have to teach our children that people who fight chickens and dogs for fun and pleasure are not to be respected or emulated, as they deserve neither.

We have to teach our children that no one looks beautiful when wearing an animal skin, but, instead, they look hideous. Only the animal wearing the skin, while living, playing, eating, sleeping, and dreaming, looks beautiful in its own fur coat.

I drove over 700 miles recently, and I had no radio in my truck. If I sing to myself it isn't at all entertaining, believe me. So what do I do? Usually I just daydream, but this trip I met a fly. As I was puttering along on the freeway, I noticed a fly winging his way around the cab, pestering me by landing on the steering wheel, my leg and—even a couple of times—my nose, which was a bit disconcerting. I opened the window so he could fly out, but instead he stubbornly went right to the center of the cab and hung on.

I tried unsuccessfully to swat him. Then it occurred to me. What am I doing? Why would I want to kill this fly? Just because he is fly? Because I am an "exterminator" (I hate that word)? He was just flying around waiting to get home so he can get out of the truck and do fly stuff. He wasn't deliberately annoying me.

If a dog barks, do I kill it? Of course not! If a snake wanders in my yard, do I kill it? No way! So why kill the fly?

Think about it. God created all of us, every species, with one thing in mind—Love. He did not create us so we can fight each other, argue with each other, barbecue each other, or swat flies! His purpose was for us to love and respect each other, and that includes every species. Would Jesus ever hunt or attend a bullfight or stomp on a bug or swat a fly? I don't think so.

Many species of animals feed on other species and that is the way of the world, for better or worse. Very few animals die of old age. However, have you ever seen a lion hang an antelope's head in his den to show how brave he is? Have you ever seen a roadrunner kill a rattlesnake and then skin it and make it into a headband for his stupid cowboy hat? No.

They kill to eat or to defend themselves or their families; they don't kill for pleasure. That is solely a human trait, purportedly because we are able to "reason." Would a monkey or a lion or a chicken or any other species of animal swat a fly simply because it is a fly? I don't think so. We don't like flies because they are bugs, and to many humans, bugs are inherently evil.

If you don't believe me, simply look at the very huge pesticide industry which spends billions of dollars polluting our planet and making people sick—all so we can kill a few bugs. I've slept in beds knowing bed bugs were present, and they happily dined on my body while I slept. I got up and went about my business the next day while the bugs slept in, fat and happy. No harm was done, yet we have created a massive industry to "control" these so-called pests (who don't carry any diseases).

There is one thing that every species of animal on the planet, including man, has in common. We are all here to simply make a living, in whatever way that means to us. Man is the only species that likes to take advantage of other species and torture them, hunt them, fish for them, spray pesticides on them, and God only knows what else. I learned a lot from little Dasher, the fly (because he liked to hang out on the dashboard). God was obviously in the truck with me that night because not only did I learn some good moral teachings from an insect, but I was driving over 150 miles at night with no taillights (which I didn't know weren't working). I could have had a serious accident or a serious citation, but God was with me all the way. When I got home and opened the door, the fly woke up and joined his buddies outside to carouse the night-life (or whatever it is flies do at night).

I learned more from that fly than I ever would have from some radio talk show host.

COCKFIGHTING

I'll leave you with this one last animal issue that really frosts my pumpkin. For a while I had a special interest in understanding the motivation behind cockfighting. As I mentioned earlier, Holly and I met on cockfighter discussion boards, where we were both eavesdropping on what they were saying and planning in an effort to put a stop to it. Cockfighters, in my opinion, are the scum of the earth, right down there with dogfighters and bullfighters.

I feel a need to include some information on cockfighting in this book because it is so inherently evil.

"You want to stop me from fighting my chickens that I hatch from my eggs? What about big money interests in New York who fight Black men? They call it boxing. Just Look at that pathetic Mohammad Alie...he can't complete a sentence...had is brains beat out.....Oh and the rapist, what is his name? You know the one ...Mike Tyson...Another Scholar....So.....It's ok to fight blacks, but don't allow us to fight our chickens? You got no concept of freedom"—A

Cockfighter

When I wrote a column on cockfighting, the letter above was one of the first I got from the pro-cockfighting people. They call themselves "cockers". As you can see, the argument is patently silly, and many of the reasons I got for legalizing cockfighting are equally idiotic.

Cockfighting dates back to a pre-Christian era. In some places, roosters were objects of worship. The ancient Syrians worshipped fighting roosters as a deity and the ancient Greeks and Romans associated the roosters with some of their gods, including Apollo, Mercury, and Mars. In parts of Indonesia, the rooster was worshipped and rituals were performed to honor the deity. Cockfighting occurred in temples and the losing bird would be placed in a golden cauldron, soaked in gums and spices, and burned on the altar. The ashes would be placed in a golden urn.

Nowadays cocks that lose fights are relegated to a dumpster. The cockers have no use for birds that lose.

During the time of Moses, in Egypt, cockfighting was very popular, and it flourished in England in the 16th century. During the reign of King Henry VIII, cockfights were held in Whitehall Palace. At its height of popularity, the clergy supported cockfighting. Finally, common sense prevailed and Queen Victoria, in the 17th century, banned cockfighting with a royal decree. It is now almost non-existent in present day England.

What is the truth about cockfighting? The following facts are from the Humane Society of the United States.

"The cruelty to birds used for cockfighting is appalling. With inches-long gaffs-needle-sharp, ice pick-like weapons-attached to their natural leg spurs, roosters are thrust into small arenas, called pits. There, trained to fight and often drugged with stimulants such as strychnine and methamphet-amines, they plunge and slash at each other. The gaffs inflict deep puncture wounds. Wings and legs are broken. Eyes are gouged out. Within minutes, the birds may be staggering from their injuries. But they are forced to fight on. Handlers pick up the birds and blow on their faces to revive them. If a bird has suffered a puncture wound to his lungs and is drowning in his own blood, his handler may suck blood from his lungs through his beak to force him to keep fighting.

When the fighting begins to flag, the birds in the main pit are removed to a drag pit. There their match may continue for hours, as their handlers revive them time and again to keep the fighting and the bets going. According to an investigator for The Humane Society of the United States (HSUS), "Even if one bird is half dead, the handlers don't stop the fight. The bird may be bleeding, stunned, and wounded, but he will be kept fighting, even if he can only lie there in fear and terror while the other bird keeps attacking him." Matches generally end only when one of the birds is wounded beyond revival.

However, the "winner," who is usually dying from his inju-ries, may face even more torture. Survivors whose eyes have been gouged out, slashed, or blinded are pitted together in "blinker derbies." Other wounded birds are thrown en masse into a "battle royale," a fight to the last bird, while spectators gamble on the outcome. At the end the birds are tossed on "dead piles"—but they are not always dead. For example, dur-ing one raid an HSUS investigator found ten birds that were still alive in a dead pile.

Cockfighters argue that the bird's aggression is natural. But in nature, roosters seldom fight to the death. Cockfight-ing birds are cruelly trained and often drugged to fight, and they are armed to fight. Finally, they are forced to fight. HSUS investigators have witnessed birds jumping out of the pit to escape their captive adversaries only to be caught and returned to the fight by the handlers, or have their heads pulled off for committing an act of "cowardice." Who, truly, are the ruthless, aggressive killers?

Not only is cockfighting barbaric, vicious, and cruel, but also evidence is overwhelming that cockfighting is linked to other crimes and violence. Law enforcement officials have documented the strong connection between cockfighting, illegal gambling, and large-scale manufacturing and distribution of illegal drugs. In many cases, law-enforcement officials have uncovered evidence of cockfighting-birds, pits, and equipment-while pursuing drug investigations and raids. Drug dealers use connections made at cockfights for the distribution of drugs. Cockfighting involves multiple crimes.

Making and watching animals suffer and die for "entertainment" is abhorrent to a civilized society. A stand against cockfighting is a stand for a society that protects animals against human cruelty and abuse. In the United States, cockfighting is illegal in every state, but it is still carried on in many areas of the country.

I thought you might want to see a few more letters from cockers defending their "sport". You can take them for what they're worth. Note that I deliberately leave in their misspellings and grammar errors for you to understand the level of intelligence we're talking about.

"Boy i think i have never read so much bolony in a life time. If you know what youre talking about fine i can acept it,but every single coment i read was so of to the left that its amazing the peoples names werent (PETA,ALF,HSUS

etc,etc.)

"Oh your going to save the world be stopping cock fighting ? you probley never attended a cock fight. and you sure don't understand a cock fight. do you understand these birds fight naturally? thats what they where invented for 1000's of years ago. king's and queen's attended cock fights. i have fowl and yes we fight them !!!! we fight them proudly. my whole family goes and watches. these fowl are well taken care of 365 days a year. you say cock fighting is cruel ? it's a way of life for a game bird.

"I can,t figure out why the people that write all the negitive article about cockfighting have never researched cockfighting, or even been to the fights. Cockfighting is a blood sport. Both roosters are equaly armed, and weigh within 3 oz. of each other. That,s as far as it gets. Take deer hunting. Thats a blood sport. Poor ole deer walking down the road, bothering nobody and a guy jumps out of the brush and shoots him. I,ll bet he did,nt want to be shot. Roosters are there because they want to be. At least give it some thought. Do your home work befor you write.".

The argument that cockfighting is not cruel because the roosters naturally fight is asinine. That's just a feeble excuse to justify what they are doing. Humans are the only species that likes to fight for no particular reason, and apparently some humans like to see animals fight. I guess because we like to participate in death and torture, other animals must like it, too. Bob Dickerman, a respected ornithologist, told me:

"In the wild Gallus gallus (the species chickens belong to) are very territorial - in the dawn in the Philippines you can hear them advertising their territories at first light calling back and forth in the deep forests of the hills, but they are all about showing off their plumage and bluff—with maybe an occasional show of force but nothing deadly. In Guatemala we would watch roosters heard their small flocks of females about, maintaining their distance from other flocks, except occasionally one rooster would dash over and have a quickie on another guy's hen, and if caught the owner would charge the intruder—but again all bluff—and a few feathers might fly, but it was nothing serious. In the wild their spurs are less than an inch long and are blunt."

The cockfighters' argument that roosters are naturally aggressive is simplistic and does not address the facts about the rooster's natural behavior. One of the reasons cockfighters give for legalizing their "sport" is because it's a tradition. In many cases a tradition includes a man's inclination to subjugate women, children and animals. In many societies women are raped, beaten, enslaved as sexual toys, exploited as wives, sold for money, used for entertainment and cheap labor, and subjugated in other ways that defy the imagination—but are still considered "traditions". In these same societies, women and animals are considered inferior, evil, and mere playthings to misuse and abuse.

Another reason cockfighters use to justify their activities is that it is biblical and God is a cockfighter. This is pure nonsense and I firmly believe these people who fight and kill chickens in cockfights are actually practitioners of Voodoo, a religion where chickens are routinely slaughtered. To show the idiocy of the religious argument the chicken fighters use, I would like to share a letter I got from one of their more eloquent members.

> *"Hey man. what are you tryin to do. you can't stop us form cockfigthing. it is a fact of the bible. i am a preacher and i know my bible. God gives humans dominos over all other animals. we can do waht we want as we see fit. cockfigthing has been aroun since Moses and it will be around when Jesus comes back. i can say you better not be aroun when Jesus gets back or you are goin to hell. cockfigthing is a kings sport. God made women and chickens for mens plesure. thats why we hav more ribs then women an brians that chickens. obvously you dont have any brians or you would read the bible and know cockfigthing is Gods chosen sport. You aint goin to rite no cockfigthing book about us an try to make us look stuped. God aint goin to alow it. you are a fool and a commie lovin homosexal and you goin to hell. the bible says so."*

It may be hard to believe, but this is a real letter, just as I received it. The only thing I took out was his religion, which I deleted so as not to embarrass normal people who might go to the same church as this fellow.

Cockfighting is a tradition and/or a religious experience? All I can say to that is – NONSENSE!

Here is another intelligent letter;

> *"I kinda like to lay it allllllllllll out every once in*

Awhile.. Just to let them know they Make NOTTA differ-ence in the Way I run my animals. I am KING over those animals and I raise Soley to Fight the feathers off of them. And every time they THINK they've made a difference I just Kick the cat right off the poarch. Millions of baby FIGHTING CHICKENS were hatched out this Year for the SOLE purpose of FIGHTING and Wages among men will take place. It is a RIGHT we have an No Man can take this away from us. I am KING of this Flock. Yea, I stick it alllllllllll out sometimes just to let them Know thier efforts are for NOTTA.. There is a couple of them getting Rich off the rest of them, and at thier expense. I think I'm gonna get the BB gun and cull out some pullets today.. A good ole glass of tea and some target practice."

I wrote frequent columns for the Daily Lobo on campus, and when I wrote one about cockfighting before it became illegal in New Mexico, it went viral and I got a lot of feedback from chicken Nazis (I mean cockfighters). These comments about my article were posted on one of their discussion boards:

"I would say this idiot also supports gun control and freeing rapists and child molestors. He sounds like your typical draft-dodging,treehugging,liberal whineass Ellen Degenneras(not sure of the spelling, and really don't give a damn)loving homosexual to me. I would like to know."

"Hey Richard, your'e still a fruitcake and a liar in my Dictionary. All I can say to you Richard is to get a life. Or

maybe get a hobby like testing hand granades or something like that.... Have a good day. (Not!!!!)"

"Notice how most of this liberal propaganda comes out of universities? I really worry these days if I should try to send my kids to be educated in these sesspools. Of course my kids tell me things that get said in public school and it is about the same speed. Folks we got to stay in touch with our children and educate them in what is right and wrong, if we do not one day they will come home and tell us how evil we are, I promise."

Not all the mail I've received on the subject has been negative nonsense from chicken fighters. I got plenty of mail from normal people with good hearts. This is one of my favorites:

"I have a comment about cockfighting. I won't even get into the issues of "culture", "tradition", and all that malarkey. The truth is that the poor roosters that are raised to fight are wonderful, intelligent creatures. We rescued one several years ago. He was "thrown away" or escaped in an ally near our house. We found him struggling to get into a trash can for food. When we picked him up and brought him home, we saw that his wing was ripped off, one of his eyes was missing, a few of his toes were gone, his combs were cut off, and he had the walk of one who wears blades. A good 'ol boy told us he was probably fed gunpowder too, because once in a while he would "go nuts". But, good 'ol Brooster was a survivor. With a little TLC he became the "king" of the backyard. He fell in love with a little white

cat and would follow her everywhere, and he'd actually lay down and sleep beside her. The dogs respected him. He would come when you called him because he knew that his own personal "produce section" was going to have fresh veggies dumped into it. He begged at the outside table with the dogs, and hung around the barbeque grill when someone was cooking. He was the sweetest, most loving, and beautiful rooster I've ever known. His retirement lasted for four years before we lost him to a bacterial infection. I still miss him, and am still disgusted at the cruelty that poor thing endured at the hands of those cockfighters."

Another big reason (as if we need more) to end cockfighting is its link to the spread of avian flu. The losing roosters are tossed in a dumpster, but the winners—who may become infected by avian flu from the transfer of blood and other body fluids during a fight—can spread the disease to other chickens they come in contact with, or even humans. Secondly, the cockfighters have the disconcerting (and disgusting) habit of clearing blood and mucous from the roosters air passageways during a fight by putting their mouth over the beak and sucking out the blood and mucous. One young cockfighter in Thailand died after sucking the mucous out of an infected rooster. According to WHO Disease Outbreak News, this was a risk factor they hadn't previously considered.

It's bad enough if a cockfighter gets the avian flu from sucking the snot out of his rooster, but worse yet that they can then pass the disease on to normal people. Why would they suck the mucous out of the birds? I guess when you bet the rent money, you want to make sure your rooster doesn't run out of steam before he is sliced and diced before a bloodthirsty audience participating in a satanic event.

Bah, obviously this issue still gets me worked up! Even though cockfighting is now illegal everywhere in the United States, I know it's still going on, which is very frustrating to me and others who care about these defenseless animals who are being used and abused for the entertainment of humans.

SECTION TWO

AN EARTH-FRIENDLY GUIDE TO PEST MANAGEMENT FOR YOUR HOME AND GARDEN

CHAPTER NINE

COLONY COLLAPSE DISORDER IN HONEY BEES

"If the bee disappeared off the surface of the globe then man would only have four years of life left. No more bees, no more pollination, no more plants, no more animals, no more man."—**Albert Einstein**

Why are bees dying in large numbers? There are several reasons. Some beekeepers undoubtedly use miticides to control the Varroa mites. One miticide, spiromesifen/spirodiclofen, is probably very toxic to bees and some beekeepers may be using this against the mites because the mites are resistant to almost every registered miticide available. Another cause could be the systemic pesticide imidacloprid. Systemic pesticides can work their way through a plants system and settle in the nectar, which is then stored in the honey by bees. The bees in turn will be feeding on contaminated honey.

nother factor is the practice of broadcast spraying of pesticides. When pesticides are sprayed on trees, shrubs or other plants, the residual chemicals can be picked up by the bees when they land on the plants. This is especially a problem when pest control companies spray trees on windy days, which is not only illegal, but also irresponsible. Even though the active ingredients in the pesticides may be considered safe for bees, the inert ingredients, which compose most of the product (up to 99% in some cases), may be severely detrimental to these insects. Not only are the inert ingredients not listed on the pesticide labels, many haven't even been tested and are classified as "toxicity unknown".

It is a fact that honey bees have been used to detect land mines because they are attracted to some component of the explosives used in the mines. The chemical structure of the highly dangerous explosive, TNT, or TriNitroToluene, which is used in land mines is benzene, toluene and other chemicals.

Benzene and toluene, two components of TNT are also inert ingredients used in many pesticides. I believe the bees are attracted to pesticides containing these inert ingredients as they are to TNT. They actually pick this material up and bring it back to the colony where they can contaminate their fellow bees and the honey they feed on.

Why should we be concerned about honey bees anyway? They are just another bug that can sting us. Wrong! Honey bees are one of the most vital species of insects on the planet. They pollinate scores of different kinds of crops such as cucumbers, squash, watermelons, apples and other fruit as well as many other important plants. They also pollinate clover, a common feed for cattle, so they are indirectly supporting our beef industry.

Unless you suffer from allergic reactions to bees, there is no reason to fear them. Honey bees are not out flying about looking for people to sting. You have to work at it to get stung by them. They are usually of a very peaceful nature and will not sting unless provoked. A honey bee stinger is a barbed ovipositor connected to the bee's poison sac. Because it is barbed, the stinger, along with the poison sac and parts of the abdomen, are pulled out of a honey bee when she stings, causing the bee to die. Thus, the honey bee sacrifices her life when she stings someone.

There is no doubt that our existence will be severely threatened if we kill off the bees. I think we need to get the Environmental Protection Agency (EPA) to require that all inert ingredients be listed on a pesticide label and that all pesticides that contain benzene or toluene be prohibited from use outdoors until this mystery can be solved. It is not up to the public to prove that these pesticides are responsible for CCD, but it is the responsibility of the pesticide industry to prove they aren't culpable in the bee decline.

I am not suggesting we do away with pesticides. Certainly there is nothing wrong with spraying around the perimeter of your home to prevent insects from coming in. Pesticides, in this case, can be beneficial as long as they are used responsibly. However, we need to get away from spraying large areas of trees and shrubs with pesticides, spraying large areas of cotton and other crops and stop spraying pesticides for mosquitoes, which probably kills many more bees than it does mosquitoes, and quit using herbicides in large areas. Herbicides are produced to kill plants, but they may have the same inert ingredients as insecticides and can be very harmful to bees.

Another reason for the population decline in honey bees is electromagnetic radiation that is emitted from cell phones and wireless towers. A study in Kerala, India said that installed cell phone towers caused a rapid decline in their honey bee population and that they could cause a complete collapse of the bee population in 10 years. The mobile phone companies installed towers to expand their network and the bee population declined. Dr. Sainuddin Pattazhy conducted the study and he concluded that the electromagnetic waves from the towers shorted out the navigational abilities of the worker bees so they couldn't find their way back to their hive after collecting pollen. The radiation also causes damage to their nervous system and they become unable to fly.

A study conducted at Landau University showed that when cell phones were placed near hives, the bees wouldn't return to them. Scientists believe the radiation generated by the cell phones was enough to interfere with the bees' communication system, which are movement patterns, with their hives.

I doubted the contention that cell phones were detrimental to bees when I first heard it. However, studies have shown that the electromagnetic fields have an impact on other species as well, including migratory birds which lose their orientation in the radiation. Researchers have found that robins were disoriented when exposed to a vertically aligned broadband or a single-frequency field.

Medium- and short-wave frequencies have been around for decades with no evidence of them effecting birds. But since the mobile phone networks went up, there have been more reports of birds, especially homing pigeons, getting lost.

If the electromagnetic radiation can effect birds, then there is no doubt in my mind it can effect insects as well, including honey bees. Whatever the cause of CCD in honey bees, we have to try to stop it. Along with their value as pollinators, the honey they produce is very beneficial.

Honey is produced in most of the countries of the world. Scientists of today also accept honey as a very effective medicine for all kinds of diseases.

CHAPTER TEN

COTTON VS. HEMP

Almost 35 percent of the pesticides applied to cotton in the world are applied in cotton fields in the United States. Close to $3 billion worth of pesticides are used on cotton worldwide each year, according to the Pesticide Action Network, and sales and uses of the product are increasing. Worldwide, cotton plays a vital role in the economies of several dozen countries.

73

Many of the pesticides used on cotton have been implicated in human cancer, water contamination, soil degradations and the killing off of various animals. In 1991, a train loaded with Metan sodium, which is used as a soil sterilant before planting cotton, derailed and spilled its contents into the Sacramento River, resulting in the death of every living organism in the river for 40 miles. A few years later heavy rains washed the chemical Endosulfan from cotton fields and into Big Nance Creek in Alabama and killed almost a quarter of a million fish.

On the other hand, there is a product that is much more efficient and much more valuable than cotton. That product is industrial hemp: A variety of *Cannabis sativa*, a tall annual herb of the mulberry family, native to Asia. Industrial hemp is not marijuana (*Cannabis indica*), as they are two different species of plants. Hemp does not possess any psychoactive qualities as it doesn't possess the necessary THC to get a buzz.

The cotton industry, politicians and other folks who have no idea what they are talking about would like us to believe that growing any hemp is comparable to marijuana. This is nonsense. If somebody wants to get high bad enough they will. You can get a buzz ingesting ants if you want to if you use the right species. For instance, some people have concocted unusual (to say the least) uses of harvester ants. Native Americans in southern California in the 1800s used harvester ants for both therapeutic and mind-altering purposes. They were administered both internally and externally in the treatment of rheumatism, colds, paralysis, body pains, stomachaches, and for various gynecological disorders. They were also swallowed to induce visions and acquire supernatural power in the form of a "dream helper" (or spiritual guide). If the vision was successful, the user saw an animal spirit, a personified natural force, or the spirit of a dead relative who then acted as a life-long spirit guide.

The user would take some moist down-feathers from an eagle, dip it into a jar of live ants, and 4 or 5 ants would cling to it and form a ball. The ball is then quickly swallowed, followed by 50 to 90 additional balls. When his throat was burning painfully or if the ants started crawling out of his mouth, the user knew he had taken enough ant balls. Shortly all the ants in his stomach would start stinging him at once and the resulting pain would cause him to pass out for a few hours and enter a catatonic state. It is while he is unconscious that the hallucinogenic dreams occur. When the trip is over, the user would then drink hot water to regurgitate the still-living ants.

The author and the publisher strongly recommend that no one try this as a means of getting a buzz. We will not accept responsibility for any idiot who attempts this very dangerous practice. Furthermore, we are sure that when some politician gets wind of it, they will pass a law against ingesting ants in their never-ending quest to protect us from ourselves. They may even designate all ant species as being a controlled substance.

Of course we don't recommend using harvester ants or marijuana, but to associate marijuana with industrial hemp is as silly as linking the hallucinogenic effect harvester ants can have on you with all other ants.

Colonists brought hemp seed with them to America and it was extensively grown for "homespun" During World War II hemp was subsidized by the government to be used for fiber and rope. Industrial hemp continued to be harvested in the US up to the 1950s when the lack of common sense took over in the government.

Using hemp instead of cotton would result in the use of 25% less pesticides than is currently being applied to our environment. Enormous numbers of trees would not have to be destroyed. Cotton growing is probably the largest polluter on the planet in terms of releasing pesticides into our environment since cotton occupies only 13% of the world's farmland, yet demands 25% of the pesticides used. The chemicals go into the groundwater and poisons not only the target insects but non-target organisms as well, including humans. Hemp, on the other hand, has long been considered a weed, but it does not require pesticides to grow. Unfortunately it is illegal to grow hemp in most states because of ill-informed politicians who lack common sense.

Hemp seed is more nutritious than soybeans, contains more essential fatty acids than any other source, and is second only to soybeans in complete protein. Further, hemp seed is high in B vitamins, is 35 percent dietary fiber, and does not contain THC like its relative, the marijuana plant. Hemp fiber is longer, more absorbent, and more insulative than cotton fiber.

According to the U. S. Department of Energy, hemp is a biomass fuel producer requiring the least specialized growing and processing of all plant products. The hydrocarbons in hemp can be processed into a wide range of biomass energy sources, from fuel pellets to liquid fuels and gases. Obviously, development of biofuels could significantly reduce our consumption of fossil fuels and nuclear power.

Hemp also produces more pulp per acre than timber on a sustainable basis, and can be used for making every quality of paper. Moreover, hemp paper manufacturing would reduce wastewater contamination.

By using hemp instead of cotton we could reduce our pesticide usage by 25% as well as not having to destroy countless numbers of trees. It is apparently forgotten that all herbs, including hemp, have their uses and that we were given all of the means we need on this Earth to live a good, healthy life.

Another option is organically grown cotton. No pesticides, fertilizers or defoliants are used in growing organic cotton. Organic solutions such as using compost, manure, naturally derived minerals and crop rotation eliminate the need for dangerous chemicals. Organic cotton can also be bred in different colors to eliminate the need for dye. It comes in a range of earth tones, such as rust, cream, browns and greens.

Chemically dependent cotton is no longer necessary and we should seriously look into increasing our yield of organic cotton and using industrial hemp. Growing cotton with pesticides and fertilizers certainly has more negatives than positives and if we want to live in a healthy environment, we need to re-evaluate our priorities on what we are growing.

Chapter Eleven

Spraying for Mosquitoes and Other Pests

West Nile Virus (WNV) is a potentially serious disease. According to the Center for Disease Control (CDC), "About one in 150 people infected with WNV will develop severe illness. The severe symptoms can include high fever, headache, neck stiffness, stupor, disorientation, coma, tremors, convulsions, muscle weakness, vision loss, numbness and paralysis. These symptoms may last several weeks, and neurological effects may be permanent. Up to 20 percent of the people who become infected have symptoms such as fever, headache, and body aches, nausea, vomiting, and sometimes swollen lymph glands or a skin rash on the chest, stomach and back. Symptoms can last for as short as a few days, though even healthy people have become sick for several weeks. Approximately 80 percent of people (about 4 out of 5) who are infected with WNV will not show any symptoms at all".

West Nile Virus originates in birds, particularly crows and closely related species. When the mosquito bites an infected bird and then bites a person, the virus is passed on. We have had far fewer cases since the virus first became a problem and that is because the descendants of the birds that originally carried the disease have developed a resistance to it, thus the mosquitoes biting the birds aren't picking up the virus as readily as they did four years ago.

Should we be concerned? Of course, as even a few cases can be serious, and we want to avoid them if we can. We also need to protect our horses which seem to catch the disease as well. We vaccinate our horses and encourage all horse owners to do the same.

What can we do about the mosquitoes that are biting us, even if the disease factor isn't as serious as it was several years ago? Make sure you have good screens on your windows and doors to keep mosquitoes and other insects out. Empty standing water from flower pots, buckets, barrels and similar containers. Change the water in bird baths weekly. Keep wading pools empty and on their sides when not in use. In other words, don't provide breeding grounds for the mosquitoes.

When you go outside, wear a good non-DEET mosquito repellent. Never use the DEET products that government agencies recommend as DEET (N,N-diethyl-m-toluamine) is a chemical that some people have severe reactions to. It is a fact that DEET works well as long as it is full strength. However, when it begins to weaken, it actually attracts mosquitoes and you have to put more on, which means absorbing more of the chemicals into your system. Every year one-third of the population uses insect repellents containing DEET, available in more than 230 products with concentrations up to 100%. The conclusion of one scientist who has conducted 30 years of study on pesticides, demonstrates that frequent and prolonged applications of DEET can cause neurons to die in regions of the brain that control muscle movement, learning, memory and concentration. There are very effective alternatives to DEET repellents and we should use them.

We can also wait for our state / county / city agency to come by and spray our neighborhood with a fogging unit mounted on a truck. Not a good idea. The pesticides they use to fog areas for mosquitoes are synthetic pyrethroids and they are not safe for humans or animals. This method of applying pesticides will kill dragonflies and other insects that feed on mosquitoes, but it is not all that effective against the target insect – mosquitoes. The CDC says spraying for mosquitoes from a truck is the least effective method of control. It also reduces the bat population by killing many insects they feed on.

Maybe it is time that the government agencies limit their activities to education and the use of larvicides and not try to protect the public from mosquitoes by using pesticides that may be every bit as dangerous as the bugs. Maybe we can protect ourselves and our pets by making sure there aren't any mosquito breeding places on our property and by using a good non-DEET mosquito repellent when we go outside. There are many communities around the country that no longer allow spraying, either from trucks or planes, pesticides for controlling adult mosquitoes. They do not have an unusually high rate of West Nile virus or any other mosquito-borne disease. Something to think about.

Children, for reasons we aren't sure of, seem to be less susceptible to West Nile Virus than adults, but they are more susceptible to the dangerous effects of pesticides, thus when we spray whole areas with pesticides to "control" West Nile Virus, we are actually putting our children in more danger.

CHAPTER TWELVE

THE PESTICIDE PROBLEM

"The EPA's Science Advisory Board concluded in 1990 that, when compared with dozens of other risks, pesticides presented one of the country's more widespread and severe environmental problems."

The pesticide industry defends the use of pesticides because pests in the United States kill 100 – 300 people annually. They claim people need to be protected from these hideous pests. There are over 325,000 certified commercial pest control applicators in the United States using pesticides. It is the National Academy of Science's estimate that pesticide poisoning causes over 10,000 cancer deaths every year and creates over 20,000 cancer cases. These figures don't include neurological damage, heart disease, lung damage, birth defects, miscarriages and other chronic exposure deaths.

A nationwide report has found that pesticide use in or near U.S. schools have sickened more than 2,500 children and school employees over a five-year period. The pesticide poisoning has resulted from pesticides being sprayed in schools or on nearby properties, and includes both insecticides and herbicides.

According to an article in Epidemiology: 12 (1):20-26, January, 2001, one of the largest studies of pesticides has found that pesticide use around the home can more than double the chance of a child developing neuroblastoma, which is a condition that accounts for about 10% of all childhood tumors. This is a very serious cancer as approximately 60% of children over age 1 who develop neuroblastoma do not live 3 years even when receiving radiation and chemotherapy treatments.

A similar study in Cancer: 89: 11, 2000 has shown that children who have been exposed to household insecticides and professional extermination methods within the home are three to seven times more likely to develop non-Hodgkin lymphoma compared to children who have not been exposed to pesticides. These two articles clearly demonstrate why we should never allow pesticides in schools or day-care centers.

Why are children at more of a risk than adults? There are many reasons. Children put their toys and other objects in their mouth and they often crawl on the ground and come in contact with pesticides. Children often wear fewer clothes resulting in dermal poisoning by many toxicants. Children breathe differently than adults. A one-year old child will breath 50% more air each minute relative to their body weight than adults do. This, of course, gives them the opportunity to inhale more pesticides. Children will pick up pesticides at home, at school, from their food and from being around pets who have been treated for fleas or ticks. If they live in an agricultural community where pesticides are heavily used, children are in even greater danger.

Pesticides are a mixture of chemicals used to kill, repel or otherwise control various pests, including insects, mites, rodents, birds, fish, weeds, fungi and other perceived pests. Pesticides are comprised of a number of different compounds, including the "active ingredient" and "inert ingredients" as well as other contaminants and possible pollutants.

Active ingredients are the only components of the pesticide listed on the label. These are the chemicals that kill and repel the pests. Active ingredients also contain synergists, such as piperonyl butoxide (PBO) to help the pesticide work more effectively. Piperonyl butoxide, a very commonly used synergist, can be toxic to the liver and is a possible human carcinogen. Pesticides that contain pyrethrin and pyrethroids are pesticide products that most often use piperonyl butoxide.

The inert ingredients are the carrier or sticking agent in the pesticide and may include solvents, stabilizers, surfactants, preservatives, sticking agents, spreading agents or defoamers, depending on the need of the product. Some inert ingredients are more toxic than the active ingredient in the product and often make up the largest percentage of ingredients in a pesticide product.

The *Federal Insecticide, Fungicide and rodenticide Act* (FIFRA) only requires manufacturers to list the active ingredients on the label. They allow the "inert" ingredients to be a trade secret leaving the consumer and the applicator unaware of the possible danger they are exposed to. Many inert ingredients are considered to be "hazardous pollutants", "extremely hazardous", "suspected carcinogens" and "occupational hazards."

Contaminants and other pollutants are byproducts of the manufacturing process and they can often contribute to a pesticide's toxicity.

Metabolites are the products that result when a pesticide breaks down by being exposed to air, water, soil, sunlight or other environmental factors. Often the metabolites are more toxic than the original product.

The suffix –cide, literally means to kill. Pesticide, suicide, homicide, genocide all have one thing in common—death. Are there any safe pesticides? Emphatically, no there are not. Can pesticides be used safely? Yes they can if they are used by people who are knowledgeable about the pesticide they are using and if they use the product carefully and if they have respect for the environment where the pesticide is going to be placed. Unfortunately, more often than not, the respect portion of the equation is lacking.

Children, the elderly, pregnant women, and those who have allergies, asthma, chemical sensitivities or other immune, respiratory, or neurological impairments are especially vulnerable to the toxic effects of pesticides.

How are pesticides introduced into the body? There are three main points of entry. Inhalation of the fumes of some pesticides is very common and can severely compromise a respiratory system. Pesticides are commonly absorbed by the skin (dermally) and occasionally ingested (orally). In the latter, it is often children who swallow pesticides carelessly left out in the open. Pets will frequently ingest rodenticides carelessly used by a pest control operator or a homeowner.

There can be no doubt that pesticides, including herbicides are associated with a number of public health risks. There are about 110,000 non-fatal human pesticide poisonings each year in the United States. In addition, pesticides have been linked with such human diseases as breast cancer, and extensive exposure can have adverse respiratory and reproductive problems, including asthma and sterility. Other problems can include blurred vision, dermatitis, reduced heart rate and even coma and death. Do all pesticides cause these problems? In fact, the Environmental Protection Agency has identified more than 90 pesticides as possible or suspected carcinogens (cancer causers). For farm workers who are exposed to pesticides more often then most other people, the problems can be severe. They have been diagnosed with excessive rates of certain kinds of cancer, including cancer of the stomach, cancer of the testes, prostrate cancer and brain cancer. Female farm workers have an increased rate of cervical cancer.

Where else are pesticides used? Along with being used in agriculture and on our public lands, commercial pesticide applications are frequently made to schools, offices, stores, theaters, restaurants, hotels, government buildings, hospitals, nursing homes, airplanes, buses, and almost all public buildings. Additionally, private citizens apply pesticides to their homes, gardens, lawns, and trees and/or hire a professional company to make such applications in their home or yard.

Do you have weeds outside that need spraying? According to Organic Gardening, July, 2000, Roundup is not your best choice for an herbicide. Thousands upon thousands of acres in the U. S. are sprayed annually with nearly 50 million pounds of Roundup. Tests on Roundup show adverse effects in all standard categories of toxicological testing, including medium-term toxicity, long-term toxicity and genetic damage. Sperm production in rabbits was diminished by 50 percent when they were exposed to glyphosate, the active ingredient in Roundup, in research conducted at two universities. New evidence suggests that Roundup may cause cancer. The study, published in Environmental and Molecular Mutagenesis (vol. 31 pp. 55-59, 1998), found that an unidentified chemical in Roundup caused genetic damage in the livers and kidneys of mice exposed to the herbicide. In California, where pesticide-related illness must be reported, Roundup's active ingredient, glyphosate, is the most common cause of pesticide illness in landscape workers.

Is your exterminator safe from his pesticides? Not really. According to Occupational Environmental Medicine, 56(1):14-21, 1999, male pesticide applicators are at a significantly increased risk of developing prostrate cancer than folks who do not apply pesticides regularly.

Another study published in the Journal of the National Cancer Institute, 71(1), July 1983, found that pesticide applicators employed for 20 or more years had nearly 3 times the risk of developing lung cancer and had twice the risk of developing brain cancer.

I believe it is safe to say that pesticides are far more dangerous than most pests and we have to continue to develop alternative ways of dealing with them. Some pest control companies realize this and treat accordingly. Others still prefer the old "spray and pray" method of pest control. Spray pesticides and pray it kills something. Never let an exterminator spray pesticides in your home, school or business as it is never necessary. There are many non-toxic alternatives that are much safer for you and your family.

All pesticides that are registered by the Environmental Protection Agency (EPA) are assigned a <u>Signal Word</u> that must appear on the label. This signal word is designated as a result of the product's acute-toxicity studies. These studies take into consideration various modes of exposure, including dermal, oral and inhalation and represent the pesticides product's ability to cause chronic problems such as cancer, genetic mutations, birth defects and Multiple Chemical Sensitivities (MCS). The signal words are:

- **DANGER** – Toxicity Category I
- **WARNING** – Toxicity Category II
- **CAUTION** – Toxicity Categories III & IV

The signal word "Danger" indicates the pesticide is <u>Highly Toxic.</u> It is corrosive or it can cause severe burning to the eyes and skin that can result in irreversible damage. There is also a "Danger-Poison" category that would indicate the pesticide is highly toxic if ingested, inhaled or absorbed through the skin. The signal word "Warning" indicates that the pesticide is <u>Moderately Toxic</u> if eaten, absorbed through the skin, inhaled or if it causes moderate eye or skin irritation. The signal word "Caution" indicates that the pesticide is only <u>Slightly Toxic</u> if ingested, absorbed or inhaled and if it causes mild eye or skin irritation.

Generally, pesticides with the Danger or Warning label are considered Restricted Use Pesticides. Pesticides with a Caution label are considered General Use.

Restricted Use pesticides are for sale to and use only by licensed and certified pest management professionals. Restricted Use pesticides are restricted because their use may cause adverse effects on the environment, including health problems because of their acute or inhalation toxicity.

General Use pesticides are for sale to and can be used by the general public.

There are other products that aren't pesticides that can be equally dangerous. Dr. Ann McCampbell, who wrote the piece in the Multiple Chemical Sensitivity chapter, found the following health effects for commonly used antimicrobial agents.

CHAPTER THIRTEEN

MULTIPLE CHEMICAL SENSITIVITY

Aspokesman for the National Pest Control Association contended in 1988 that many people who claim they are "chemically sensitive" are actually allergic to the pests that the chemical (poison) is supposed to control. Others, he says, have *"delusory parasitosis, a distinct fear of insects. It's a neurotic disorder of people that can never be controlled."* What do you want to bet that this person never got a medical degree?

Multiple Chemical Sensitivity (MCS) is a real disease that affects a large segment of our society. Many more people may not know they have MCS until they are exposed to pesticides or other chemicals. Sharyn Davidson worked for a veterinarian clinic and was exposed to pesticides used on our dogs and cats. This exposure triggered MCS in her. She can describe in her own words her battle with Multiple Chemical Sensitivity.

People with Multiple Chemical Sensitivity (MCS) often refer to themselves as canaries, or biological sentinels, who signal impending danger from toxic exposures. Recent epidemiological research revealed that as many as 16% of the population considers themselves sensitive to some chemicals. MCS has become like a half-ton canary that no one can any longer ignore. Many people with MCS are intolerant of pesticides, solvents, and many other synthetic products that never existed until humans created them.

Some would have you believe that there is nothing wrong with these synthetic products, but that there is something emotionally wrong with those who report reacting to these products. Can thousands and thousands of people who report intolerance to toxic chemicals be suffering from mass psychogenic illness? The opponents of MCS would like you to believe that. If designer poisons interfere with the life processes and kill life forms lower on the food chain, why is it a stretch of logic to understand that these same chemicals interfere with the life engendering metabolism of humans and make them ill?

Most people with MCS do not have antibody mediated allergies. Most toxic chemicals are not allergens. They are chemicals that interfere with the natural metabolic pro-

cesses. Immune suppressive toxins have been found in the fats of dead whales in Puget Sound and in the fat biopsies of humans with MCS, cancers and other toxic induced disorders. Unlike the highly impacted wildlife, those of us with chemical sensitivity can verbalize the emotional and physiological distress triggered by the many synthetic toxins. These supposedly "safe" synthetic chemicals created by man have reached the top of the food chain and are now creating a health crisis. Although many people appear to tolerate many of these synthetic products, there are many of us who are made ill by them.

Although we don't completely understand the mechanism of MCS, we are getting closer. We would like those who do not experience chemical sensitivity but who understand that the fragile web of our common environment has now been diminished to advocate for research to shed greater understanding of this issue. There can be no resolution of any problem without first acknowledging and understanding the problem. Please become informed about the impact of toxins on the quality of your life. The most important thing we can do is to find understanding through research and explain the mechanism of the disorder so that the problems can be resolved

My chemical sensitivity this past 19 years has been like a bad dream in which the Emperors have all their clothes on but they cannot see, hear or think clearly. In this nightmare, a small canary is yelling wake up Bellingham, dioxins are dangerous! Wake up Washington State, pesticides are poisons. Wake up America, your canaries are ill! Wake up Earth, toxic chemicals impair life! Are those of us with MCS the only ones who can see, hear, and understand the canary?

Sharyn's case clearly demonstrates that MCS is real. The following Conclusion is from an article written by Ann McCampbell and published in *Townsend Letter for Doctors and Patients*, January, 2001. Ann suffers from Multiple Chemical Sensitivity, and this is reprinted with her permission.

MCS is under siege by a well-funded and widespread disinformation campaign being waged by the chemical and pharmaceutical industries. Their goal is to create the illusion of controversy about MCS and cast doubt on its existence. These industries feel threatened by this illness, but rather than heed the message that their products may be harmful, they have chosen to go after the messenger instead. While corporations are only beholden to their stockholders, medicine and government need to be responsive to the needs of their patients and citizens. Unfortunately, industry has convinced many in the medical and legal professions, the government, the general public, and even loved ones of people with MCS, that this illness doesn't exist or is only a psychological problem. As a result, people whose lives have already been devastated by the illness itself frequently are denied appropriate health care, housing, employment opportunities, and disability benefits. On top of this, people with MCS often have to endure hostility and disrespect from the very agencies, professionals, and people who are supposed to help them.

For example, an elderly woman with MCS was forced out of public housing and became homeless when staff insisted on remodeling her apartment, even though she warned them ahead of time that the new carpet and cabinets would make her too sick to continue living there. The physician of a woman, hospitalized because she was hav-

ing anaphylactic reactions to all foods, tried to transfer her to the psychiatric ward for "force feeding." A school district fired a chemically sensitive teacher for excessive absentee-ism after it failed to provide her with the accommodations she had requested and needed in order to work. A former airline attendant had to camp in the desert and a mother and her small child had to live in their car because they could not find housing that did not make them severely ill. And a man disabled with MCS is unable to obtain vocational rehabilitation services even though he wants to work.

Countless others have failed to find tolerable housing, including a former marathon runner who has lived in her car for 7 years and struggles to fight off frostbite every winter. In another case, a chemically sensitive woman living in her trailer was forced to leave a state park when hostile staff insisted on spraying pesticides while she was there. The park supervisor said that he had seen a television show on MCS which convinced him that he did not have to make accommodations for people claiming to have MCS because it did not exist. The show had featured ESRI's then executive director and portrayed people with MCS as free-loaders and misfits.

Despite the chemical industry's disinformation cam-paign, however, and its influence over doctors, lawyers, judges, and government, incremental progress is being made with respect to MCS. This is a testament to the strength, courage, dedication, and sheer numbers of people with MCS. In fact, there are so many people becoming chemically sensitive that attempts to ignore or silence them are ultimately doomed to fail. But even though it is just a matter of time before MCS gets the recognition it deserves, *each day it is delayed prolongs the suffering of millions of people with MCS and puts millions more at risk of developing it. Therefore, it is essential that those in medicine, government, and society begin to see past the industry disinformation campaign in order to recognize the true nature of MCS and the urgent need to address this growing epidemic.*

I have seen many cases of MCS in my many years in the pest control business. This is one of the main reasons I steadfastly promote pesticide notification whenever pesticides have to be used (and they usually don't) and why I recommend natural products whenever possible.

CHAPTER FOURTEEN

INVISIBLE BITING BUG SYNDROME (IBBS)

Question: *I am being eaten alive by mites. I think these teeny-weeny, black/grey specs are bugs. I thought bed bugs but I see no blood anywhere (except on my body, where I scratch myself in the morning. (yes I put cortisone on.) There are no poop and only a few specs about this size 'I" and they are almost invisible. I have to use a lamp and glasses to see them. I also found the running my hand light-*

ly over the bedsheet in the morning allows me to feel white specs this size "," with two or three grey I's. I remove them with scotch tape. How can these teeny bugs do so much harm? What are they? My husband thinks I'm being neurotic - he doesn't have any bites nor itches and sleeps next to me. He laughs at my complaints. I am wearing perfume to bed and spreading baby powder around but no relief.

Answer: Twenty years ago I would get a call a month about someone with "imaginary" bugs crawling on them. Most pest control people would get these occasional calls as well. We called it Delusional Parasitosis (DP) and recommended a psychologist. About ten years ago the calls increased to one a week or so and now I am getting them almost on a daily basis. This is no longer a psychological problem, but a real physical problem and it is reaching epidemic proportions in this country. I coined the term Invisible Biting Bug Syndrome (IBBS) for this condition. It is also known as Morgellon's Disease (MD).

There are several possible causes of this condition and one of them may be mites. Occasionally people have pigeons or starlings or other birds nesting on their homes. If the birds leave and don't return, the mites that may be in their nest will find their way into your home and will bite the inhabitants. If you have rodents in your house, the same thing will happen if the rodent dies from poisoning or just doesn't come back to their nesting area. The rodent mites will migrate into your living area. The one bug that doesn't affect humans although it is said to do so by some companies is the springtail (Collembola). Springtails feed on decaying vegetation and do not bite or infest humans. To treat for the mites, you should fog your bedroom and any other room you suspect they may be.

To fog, utilize 1 quart Greenbug for People for up to 1200 sq ft. Starting at the far side of a room, aim the fogger directly at all potential hiding spots making sure the mist penetrates thoroughly. Pry fabric apart, point into electrical outlets, blast up under heavy furniture, fog all nooks and crannies as you move your way out of the room. Continue to direct at hiding spaces until there is a dense fog in the room. All mites will quickly die from exposure. Allow the fog to penetrate 4 hours to overnight. Never use synthetic pesticides as they can make matters worse if you react badly to the chemicals. Greenbug is made from cedar and is available online at www.greenbugall-natural.com

Another possibility is follicle mites (*Demodex* spp.) The adult mites are only 0.3–0.4 millimeter (0.012–0.016 in) long, they have a semitransparent, elongated body that consist of two fused segments. Eight short, segmented legs are attached to the first body segment. The body is covered with scales for anchoring itself in the hair follicle, and the mite has pin-like mouth-parts for eating skin cells, hormones and oils (sebum) which accumulate in the hair follicles. The mites can leave the hair follicles and slowly walk around on the skin, at a speed of 8–16 centimeters (3.1–6.3 in) per hour, especially at night, as they try to avoid light. Mating takes place in the follicle opening, and eggs are laid inside the hair follicles or sebaceous glands. The six-legged larvae hatch after three to four days, and the larvae to develop into adults in about seven days. The total lifespan of a *Demodex* mite is several weeks. The dead mites decompose inside the hair follicles or sebaceous glands.

Older people are much more likely to carry the mites; about a third of children and young adults, half of adults, and two-thirds of elderly people are estimated to carry the mites. The lower rate of children may be because children produce much less sebum. It is quite easy to look for one's own *Demodex* mites, by carefully removing an eyelash or eyebrow hair and placing it under a microscope.

The mites are transferred between hosts through contact of hair, eyebrows and of the sebaceous glands on the nose. Different species of animals host different species of *Demodex*.

In the vast majority of cases, the mites go unobserved, without any adverse symptoms, but in certain cases (usually related to a suppressed immune system, caused by stress or illness) mite populations can dramatically increase, resulting in a condition known as "Demodicosis". It can be characterized by itching, inflammation and other skin disorders. Blepharitis (inflammation of the eyelids) can also be caused by *Demodex* mites. Some evidence links *Demodex* mites to some forms of the skin disease rosacea, possibly due to the bacterium *Bacillus oleronius* found in the mites.

There are other possible causes of Morgellons. Pollutants in the air can be reacting with skin and flesh cells in some way. Pesticides may be a factor. I asked a group of folks who have MD about this and if they are exposed to pesticides. Many said they were and the few that said they weren't did admit they go into public buildings such as restaurants. Anyone who goes into any public building that uses pesticides will be exposed. While the active ingredient in the pesticide may break down, there are a number of inert ingredients (usually comprising 98% or more of the pesticide) that may be more resilient in the atmosphere. Pesticides have been linked to Parkinson's disease as well as some genital abnormalities in babies. It is perfectly logical to come to the conclusion that exposure to pesticides can cause many of the symptoms people who suffer from Morgellons are complaining about.

There is evidence coming out now that Morgellon's might

be caused from eating genetically modified (GM) foods. Go to http://www.naturalnews.com/023004.html for more information. This is going to require a lot more study, but the implication is that the chemicals in the GM foods can cause your nervous system to send messages to your brain that something is biting you or crawling on your skin. This is certainly not a psychological disorder, but a physical disorder caused by the chemicals. You may want to start eating organic foods and stay away from any GM foods if possible. Realistically it may not be possible to avoid them all as the food makers aren't required to label their foods as genetically modified at the present time. Shop at health food stores whenever possible and avoid any meat that comes from factory farms as it is loaded with chemicals. Never let pest control person spray pesticides in your home. Around the outside is fine, but not indoors where you will be exposed to it. I am convinced after studying this syndrome for many years that it is caused by chemicals in our bodies, not by bugs or fungi. Many chemicals can interact with our nerves and send false messages to our brains. For instance, some chemicals can tell our brain something is crawling on us or biting us, and then we react by scratching, and worse yet, spraying ourselves with pesticides or chemically loaded skin products, which just exacerbates the problem. Some people describe it as a feeling of bugs or parasites scuttling around beneath their skin, accompanied by open lesions that heal slowly and ooze out blue, black or white fibers that can be several millimeters long. These fibers appear like pliable plastic. They can be as fine as spider silk, yet they are strong enough to distend the skin when pulled and elicit shooting pains when you try to remove them. Some of these fibers have been analyzed and they contain along with other substances, bovine DNA. That means the chemicals causing the fibers probably came from drinking milk or eating beef from chemically fed cattle. Vitaly Citovsky, Professor of Biochemistry and Cell Biology at Stony Brook University in New York, discovered that the fibers also contain the substance Agrobacterium, a genus of gram-negative bacteria capable of genetically transforming not only plants, but also other species, including human cells.

Here is what you need to do to try to solve this problem.

First, never expose yourself to pesticides or insect repellents that contain DEET. These products have a lot of chemicals that can harm you. If you use them, they can destroy your immune system making you susceptible to other products. Don't let pesticides be applied in your home or your workplace and try not to frequent any public building like a restaurant that has recently been treated with pesticides.

Never eat meat from a factory farm. This means almost all meat found in a supermarket or Walmart. If you have to eat meat, eat only meat from small farms or ranches. Never eat vegetables or fruits that have been sprayed with pesticides. If the vegetables and fruits don't say 100% Organic on the label, don't eat them.

Don't eat any food that contains genetically modified organisms (GMOs). One expert, Jeffrey Smith, links GMOs to toxins, allergies, infertility, infant mortality, immune dysfunction, stunted growth, and death.

Don't consume anything that contains aspartame, such as Equal or Nutrasweet. As a result of its unnatural structure, your body processes the amino acids found in aspartame very differently from a steak or a piece of fish. The amino acids in aspartame literally attack your cells, even crossing the blood-brain barrier to attack your brain cells, creating a toxic cellular overstimulation called excitotoxicity. Also wheat, dairy, and soy contain exceptionally high levels of glutamic and aspartic acid, which makes them all potentially excitotoxic. It is quite possible these chemicals are communicating false messages to your brain, indicating biting bugs that aren't there.

Don't eat food out of cans or drink water or other beverages from plastic bottles. The lining of most metal cans has a thin plastic liner that contains bisphenol-A. Bisphenol-A, or BPA, is a chemical thought to increase the risk of infertility, cancer, diabetes, and even heart disease. This chemical is also in plastic bottles. While bisphenol-A may not be directly related to IBBS, it is a chemical that can have a adverse affect on people. There is no reason to weaken your immune system with any chemicals that can be avoided.

Avoid cotton products if at all possible, particularly tampons if you are a woman. In the United States alone, approximately 600 thousand tons of pesticides and chemical fertilizers are applied to cotton fields each season. To bring this fragile plant to harvest, it is heavily sprayed 30 to 40 times a season, in extreme cases, with pesticides so poisonous they gradually render fields barren. Some of this cotton is used to make furniture, mattresses, tampons, swabs, and cotton balls. The average American woman will use 11,000 pesticide treated tampons or sanitary pads during her lifetime. Use only natural tampons.

Don't use cleaning products such as soaps that contain triclosan or triclocarban. These chemicals are endocrine disrupters. They are widely used in antibacterial soaps, body washes, lip glosses, deodorants, dog shampoos, and even toothpastes. Some brands that contain them are Dial, Colgate, Lever 2000 and Vaseline.

There is no guarantee that avoiding all of these products will solve your problem, but it certainly may help. It may take awhile for the chemicals to be removed from your system, so don't expect an overnight reaction. You may have to give it several months before you see the symptoms of IBBS start to disappear.

In some cases, the symptoms may not go away. There are three possible scenarios to IBBS (or Morgellons). One could be mites in the house. If you treat the house with a non-toxic product such as Greenbug, and the problem doesn't go away, then it is most likely chemically related as stated above. If that doesn't produce results, then it is probably psychological, which is possible in rare cases.

CHAPTER FIFTEEN

BUGS IN AND AROUND THE HOME

I'm sure by now you realize that I have a strong desire and feel a responsibility to protect the creatures who share this planet with me, with all of us. Therefore, I hope you'll understand that when I write about removing pests from your home—no matter the species—it is from a recognition that sometimes there is genuine conflict and infestations in our homes and gardens which we cannot allow to happen for reasons of sanitation and disease.

I do not shallowly discuss killing any beings, whether they be cows, chickens, or ticks, which I consider among the most-dangerous pests in our country. I just ask that you too keep this in mind, and do as little harm to the planet as you can when considering which insects are truly pests and which can be ushered along without eradication.

This section is written to help everyone understand the so-called pests in their area and how to control them—IF they are really pests and not just passing through. The book is written in a scientific format using scientific entomological names for all the pests so anyone can check them out for more information if they want. It is easy for everyone to understand as well. For instance, exterminators often tell people they have little black ants because the ants in their house are small and black. That could be any of several common pests, including *Tapinoma sessile, Monomorium minimum* or *Tetramorium caespitum*.

In some cases I will lump several closely related pests together as their habits are the same. In these cases I will only use the generic name followed by spp., which means several species. For instance, *Crematogaster* spp., means there are several species of acrobat ants that are household pests. Some insect common names make sense, like the harvester ants, which harvest seeds. Others like the acrobat ants are stupid. Ants don't work in circuses. Pavement ants are well named because they live under concrete slabs in a home. Big-headed ants are not well named because 90% of the big-headed ants have normal-sized heads!

All groups of insects will be followed by their scientific Order name such as Ants (Hymenoptera). Families will also be noted so the reader can see the relationship between different insects. Formicidae is the family of ants. All family names end in "idae". Subfamilies are smaller groups within a family.

There are three subfamilies of ants in the book, Formicinae, Myrmicinae and Dolichoderinae. All subfamily names end in "inae". The reader can Google any of the entomological names and find more information on the insect they are interested in.

I am also providing a lawn and ornamental pest management section. In this section I describe the habits of each bug and what they infest, as well as list some control methods. I furnish recipes for some pest management solutions—not all of these recipes are scientifically tested, but people have said they work, so feel free to give them a try.

Scientific testing is important in some areas, but not necessarily in pest management. I know that beer and masking tape work in controlling cockroaches and I am pretty sure they have not be tested by any university.

I want to drive home the point that most people can recognize and control their own pests without using pesticides—there are only a few cases where they will need to use an exterminator.

There are really good companies in the pest control industry and quite a few more that just aren't good. This includes the "spray and pray" people who like to spray pesticides and pray it kills something. We need to eliminate this group from our homes and this business. I include some tips for hiring a competent pest management company.

What is a pest? A pest is an organism so designated by the pesticide industry to promote the use of their chemicals. In reality, most so-called "pests" are nothing more than nuisances we occasionally encounter in our homes or business. Bed bugs don't carry any diseases and are not dangerous, but they are one of the most profitable "pests" on the planet. In reality, they are nothing more than a nuisance you may end up sleeping with some night. Cockroaches are described by the pesticide industry as being filthy disease-laden bugs that will make you sick. Except in a few cases in ghetto-type environments, that is not the case at all. Call your local hospital and ask them how many people they treat due to cockroach related diseases. None.

Ants are a mere nuisance in most cases, but some species like fire ants can be dangerous and should be considered a pest. Some other species, such as Argentine ants that have enormous colonies and can overrun a house should also be considered pests. Most species can be controlled with simple baiting solutions.

There are other real pests such as certain species of mosquitoes that can carry diseases. Some fleas and ticks can also carry diseases. Some rodents not only carry diseases such as hantavirus, but carry ectoparasites that can cause problems for humans. Termites can do serious damage to your home and some insects will destroy clothing or get into food. These all can and should be considered pests. But most of the so-called "pests" we spray with dangerous pesticides are really no more than nuisances. We need to look at our household invaders and decide for ourselves: are they dangerous, or are they simply a nuisance? Then act accordingly.

Even in the case of real pests, most can be controlled without dangerous pesticides.

Chances are that no matter what you do, you will see an occasional insect or spider in your home. There are several things you can do to minimize the chances of seeing these intruders. First, proper sanitation is important. Keep debris on your property to a minimum. This includes dead leaves, mulch, wood, garbage, manure, pet feces, weeds, boxes, grass clippings, and anything else that isn't necessary and that bugs would find attractive.

Also, install door sweeps on your outside doors if they do not close tightly. If you can see light under the doors, insects can crawl in. Raise any garbage containers off the ground and place them on concrete pads, bricks or pallets. Routinely clean any gutters you may have. Inspect the outside of your house and seal or caulk any cracks in the foundation or voids abound pipes or any other areas which will give bugs access to your house.

Make sure all of your screens are in good repair. Don't let any branches from nearby trees or shrubs touch your roof, prune them back if necessary. If you live in an area where cockroaches are prevalent, make sure all of your drains are closed at night. If you don't have a drain cover, put a Ziploc bag filled with water on the drain to keep the roaches from coming up and into the house. Cockroaches are most active from 10 p.m. to 2 a.m.

COMMON HOUSEHOLD PESTS

BRISTLETAILS (THYSANURA)

Silverfish and firebrats are the only two insects from this order that become pests and firebrats are not common in homes. True bristletails (Machilidae) are almost always found outside.

Silverfish (Lepismatidae – *Lepisma saccharina*)

Silverfish are small insects, up to ¾ inch long and silvery in color. They are covered in scales, which will be hard to see with the naked eye, and they have three appendages protruding from their abdomen.

They feed on fungus, sugar and starch products such as flour, glue and paste. They can feed on some synthetic fabrics and cellulose which includes paper, books, photographs and cardboard boxes. They will also feed on dead insects. Silverfish are attracted to moisture so you want to make sure you fix any plumbing leaks as soon as possible. They are frequently found in crawl spaces under a home if it is damp there. You have to make sure no moisture is available for these insects and try to keep items such as paper, books, and food products as far from the floor as possible.

You can trap them by putting some flour in a glass jar and wrapping it with duct tape so they can climb up the sides. They will get in the jar but will not be able to get out. Niban Bait is a good commercial bait for controlling silverfish.

COCKROACHES (BLATTODEA)

First, I have to state that there is some disagreement among entomologists as to the proper name for the order of cockroaches. Sometimes they use Blatarria or Blattoptera. Some even use Dictyoptera.

You can help prevent cockroaches from coming into your home by inspecting all incoming food products, all boxes, and any used furniture or appliances for the presence of cockroaches or their egg capsules. Do not store paper bags anywhere in the kitchen. Seal any holes or crevices around plumbing, under sinks, and behind toilets. Regularly vacuum and clean floors under the kitchen appliances. Keep all of your drains closed at night to prevent them from coming up from the sewer system. Also, get your attic and crawlspace, if you have one, dusted with food-grade diatomaceous earth.

There are a number of good baits available for controlling

cockroaches. You can put equal amounts of baking soda and sugar out in flat containers and they will take it. Make a roach dough by combining ½ c. powdered sugar and ¼ c. shortening or bacon drippings. Add ½ c. onions, ½ c. flour and 8 oz. baking soda. Add enough water to make a dough-like consistency. Make balls of bait and put them wherever you see roaches. However, there is a very good roach bait available commercially. It is Niban Bait and it is made from boric acid. It would probably be easier to get this product and use it if you are in an area where roaches are very common. You can't buy Niban in stores, but it is available online. One good supplier is www. pestcontrolsupplies.com. When using Niban, put it under and behind appliances, around hot water heaters, inside lower cabinets, in the garage and other places roaches will hide.

German roaches, Oriental roaches, Australian and American roaches all originated in North Africa. German and Oriental roaches traveled on Phoenician or Greek vessels to Asia Minor and areas around the Black Sea. Then they moved from Russia to Western Europe and eventually to America. It is thought the American cockroaches came to America from Africa on slave ships.

American cockroaches (Blattidae - *Periplaneta americana*)

This common roach feeds on a wide variety of plant and animal material and it is commonly found in sewer systems. It will come up the drains at night and enter the living space of a home. It also likes the homes that have crawl spaces under them. In some parts of the country, particularly the southeast, they frequently live outside. The is the largest of the home-infesting roaches in the country. It will reach a little over 1 ½ inches in length. It is a dark brown with yellowish band around its thorax (section behind head).

One beneficial aspect of this cockroach is that it will feed on bed bugs. Of course most people don't want roaches in their bed feeding on the bed bugs that are feeding on the humans. Niban Bait is a very good commercial bait that works well on controlling these insects. Other methods of control are discussed above. American roaches are called "Palmetto Bugs" in Florida. They can fly unlike most roaches.

Australian cockroaches (Blattidae -*Periplaneta australasiae*)

The Australian cockroach is similar to the American cockroach, but is slightly smaller. The yellow markings on the thorax are much more distinct on this roach and it has a yellowish marking on the outer edge of each wing or the "shoulder". It is found from central Florida to east Texas in the south. It has been found in some northern states, but usually in greenhouse environments. They normally infest the attics and crawl spaces of homes and then wander in the living areas for food. I would suggest dusting attics and crawl spaces with food-grade diatomaceous earth. Niban Bait works well with these roaches.

Oriental cockroaches (Blattidae - *Blatta orientalis*)

Oriental cockroaches or "waterbugs" are found throughout the United States but they aren't seen very often in the southeastern states. They are about an inch long. The female is all black and the male has two brown wing tips, but it cannot fly. These roaches are common in sewer systems and will come up the drains into the homes. They are also common under ground debris outside and love stacks of firewood. These roaches will readily take Niban Bait as well as the homemade baits discussed above.

Turkestan cockroaches (Blattidae - *Blatta lateralis*)

Turkestan cockroaches are closely related to Oriental roaches. They are about in inch in length with color variations between the male and female. Males are red/brown with pale or white lateral stripes on the ventral side of the wing base. The male also has wings that cover the entire abdomen. Females are dark brown in color with short lateral white dashes at end of the wing. The female wings are very short in comparison to the male and do not cover the entire abdomen. They are common in north Africa and the Middle East and probably came to America with military personnel returning from that area in the 1970s and 1980s. Although they are found in the southwest from California to Texas, they usually do not infest homes. They can be found in sewer systems, water meters, compost piles, potted plants and large cracks in pavements. Niban Bait is a good product for controlling these insects.

Brown-banded cockroaches (Blatellidae - *Supella longipalpa*)

Brown-banded cockroaches are about a half inch long. Males are light brown while the female has dark brown wings. Both sexes have light colored bands running across the wings. These roaches do not require as much water as German roaches and will often be found in bedrooms and living rooms. The roach baits described above will work on these insects.

German cockroaches (Blatellidae - *Blatella germanica*)

The German cockroach is the most prolific of the roaches. It is small, dark brown with two distinct black stripes on its thorax. It will feed on almost anything edible and a lot of things we wouldn't consider edible. They go from egg to adult in as little as 45 days and, if left unchecked, can severely infest a home or business. Usually they are most commonly found in kitchens and bathrooms. When you are controlling German roaches, you should use German Roach Pheromone Traps as well as some of the baits. The traps will attract and catch the roaches. They are available online. One good supplier is www. pestcontrolsupplies.com.

German cockroaches are also believed capable of transmitting *staphylococcus, streptococcus* and *coliform* bacteria and are known to be responsible for many allergy and asthma problems. In addition, German cockroaches have been implicated in the increase of asthma and the spread of typhoid, AIDS, dysentery and leprosy organisms. Living roaches, dead roaches, roach feces, saliva, cast skins, cockroach eggs and their decaying body parts all contain allergens, can contaminate the air with aeroallergens and cause allergic reactions in people.

ANTS (HYMENOPTERA – FORMICIDAE)

There are more than 20,000 species of ants around the world and about 570 species in the United States. Of those, about 30 species are common household pests. When discussing ants, we will use three terms that reflect the size of the ants in a colony. If ants are "monomorphic", it means all the workers are the same size. If they are "bimorphic", they have two sizes in the colony. The larger ones are major workers and the smaller ones are minor workers. If they have three or more sizes of workers in the colony, they are considered "polymorphic".

There are several things you can do to prevent ants from entering your home. The first step is exclusion. Go around the outside of your home and inspect it very carefully from an ant's point of view. Ants can sense cool air and aromatic odors emanating from your home and will try to gain access. Check around the house at ground level and look for cracks in the foundation, voids around pipes, areas under stucco, peepholes in bricks and similar areas that ants can use to gain entrance. All these areas need to be sealed, caulked, screened or otherwise altered to prevent ants from using them to get into your home. Check around your windows and doors to make sure they close tightly. If the doors aren't tight, you may have to install door sweeps on them. Check your bushes, shrubs and trees to make sure you don't have any branches touching the roof. Don't stack firewood, bricks or anything else next to your house or ants and other insects may find a good place to nest. If you have bushes or shrubs next to your house, periodically inspect them for aphids, scales and similar bugs, as ants are attracted to the honeydew they produce. Don't put flagstone or flat boards on the ground too close to your home or some species of ants will nest under them. On the other hand, mound-making ants will generally stay outside. They rarely leave their complicated and efficient home life in the mound to enter homes. If you don't want the ants making mounds in your yard, you can flood the nests with club soda or with white vinegar or food-grade diatomaceous earth (DE). If you use the DE, mix 4 tablespoons per gallon of water. You can also use 1 gallon of orange juice diluted with 2 gallons of water and a dash of soap. If you prefer, you can also spread dry instant grits on the mound. The ants will eat it and not be able to digest it and die.

You can repel ants with a wide variety of products, including cinnamon, baking soda, Comet cleanser, cedar oil, medicated baby powder, Tide, talcum powder, chalk, coffee grounds, borax, garlic, broken egg shells, bone meal, black or red pepper, peppermint, paprika, chili powder and mint leaves.

If you have ants going into your hummingbird feeder, you can put duct tape, sticky side out, on the wire holding the feeder, to deter them.

The best way to control them when they get in your home is with baits. Different species have different food preferences. Some species will take a wide variety of baits, while others are more fussy.

You can use a bait containing half baking soda and half powdered sugar and place it where you see foraging ants.

You can also use instant grits, which they can't digest or use 2 packets of Equal or NutraSweet, which contains aspartame, wherever you see the ants.

If the ants have a preferred food in your home, such as apple sauce, peanut butter, canned cat food, Karo Syrup, jelly or similar products, you can mix in small amounts of boric acid or borax or aspartame. Mix about 2% of any of these products in the food. Make sure you keep these baits away from children and pets. If the ants are dying near the baits, you are making it too strong and need to make a fresh batch with less boric acid or borax.

Here is a recipe for effective, homemade ant baits/traps that use borax. It attracts ants looking for either moisture or food. You will need: 3 c. water, 1 c. sugar, 1 tsp. borax or 2 tsp. food-grade DE or aspartame, 6 small screw-top jars with lids, such as jelly jars covered with masking tape, which will enable the ants to climb up the side. Mix the sugar, water and borax (or food-grade DE or aspartame) in a bowl. Loosely half-fill the jars with cotton balls or pieces of sponge or wadded paper towels. Pour up to ½ cup of the sugary mixture over the cotton balls, saturating them. Make several small holes in the lid. Screw the lids on the jars tightly.

If you smoke, always wear plastic gloves when making ant baits or they will sense the tobacco smoke on the baits and not go to it. Ants do not like cigarette or cigar smoke.

If you are finding ants in a classroom or office building and baits aren't practical, then you can spray all of the foraging ants with Greenbug for Indoors, which is a cedar product and will kill the ants it hits and repel others. Here are some of the ants most likely to be encountered in your home or yard.

There are three groups (Subfamilies) of ants that have pest (or guest) species. They are Myrmicinae, Dolichodorinae and

Formicinae.

Big-headed ants (Myrmicinae - *Pheidole* spp.)

Big-headed ants are bimorphic seed gatherers. The minor workers look like average ants. They gather the seeds and the major workers, with the enlarged heads, break them open. The major workers also defend the colony. These ants usually have small colonies of a couple of hundred individuals. Occasionally they will come in a house and make a nuisance of themselves by their presence. They won't hurt anything. Niban Bait is effective in controlling them.

Acrobat ants (Myrmicinae - *Crematogaster* spp.)

Crematogaster are commonly called "acrobat ants". This is a bit silly as they don't do anything acrobatic except occasionally running around on four legs instead of all six. Acrobat ants are small, usually red and black, but there are all black species as well. The abdomen (last segment) appears flat on top when viewed from the side and is spade-shaped when viewed from above. There are two small spines on the thorax (segment between the head and abdomen). Acrobat ants are found over most of the United States. These ants are monomorphic.

Acrobats normally feed on the honeydew secretion of aphids and related insects that infest plants near your home. They may enter your home from the roof if there are any branches touching the house or from the ground. They will get between vigas and latillas in some homes and kick out a lot of loose sawdust. It looks like they are doing damage, but they aren't. They are simply making a mess.

They will readily take sweet baits. You can make a bait with honey or Karo Syrup mixed with 2% boric acid or borax. Terro Ant Bait is also very good.

Little black ants (Myrmicinae - *Monomorium minimum*)

This species is commonly called "little black ants", which is confusing as there are several species of little (small) black ants. *Monomorium minimum* are very small, shiny black ants that are monomorphic. These ants are found throughout the United States and southern Canada. Usually they nest out-doors where they can feed on the honeydew secretion of some insects, but occasionally they infest homes. In a home they will eat whatever is available, including bread, meats, sweets, fruits and vegetables. They will bite to protect themselves. They can be controlled using a bait made from two tablespoons each of peanut butter and jelly mixed with one tablespoon of boric acid or borax. Outside you can treat any nests with Greenbug for Outdoors, which is a cedar product.

Pharaoh ants (Myrmicinae - *Monomorium pharaonis*)

This species is commonly called "pharaoh ants". They are very small, yellowish ants that are monomorphic. They got their name because they were originally discovered and described in Egypt in 1758, but are found in many areas of the United States. They will nest in any small, dark voids; such as old boxes, empty bags, stacked newspapers, under flooring, and/or especially near hot water pipes or heating systems. Outdoors they will nest under objects on the ground, in potted plants, in stacked firewood, or piles of bricks. They are primar-ily nocturnal and mainly come out to feed at night.

They have very large colonies, often exceeding a quarter

of a million ants, with a couple hundred queens. They do not swarm to reproduce as most ants do, but using a system called "budding." This is where reproductives just crawl off and mate nearby. Colonies of pharaoh ants usually contain many nests and it is essential to control all of them or you will never get rid of them. Never use synthetic pesticides in trying to control these ants as all you will do is cause them to split up and you will make the problem worse. Place baits such as half and half fruit juice and aspartame in soda straws. Cut the straws into one inch segments and put the segments where you have seen the pharaoh ants foraging. You can even tape them to the underside of tables. You can change the baits periodically by mixing peanut oil, sweet syrup, jelly or honey with 3% boric acid or food grade diatomaceous earth. Place the straw filled baits as close to the nests as possible. You can also put strained liver baby food, honey or peanut butter mixed with 2% boric acid or borax in small cups. Treat any cracks and crevices around the outside of the home with Greenbug for Outdoors.

Pharaoh ants are a major pest in hospitals, where they have been associated with over 20 disease-causing pathogenic organisms. They often enter isolation wards, operating rooms, and patient rooms where they feed on blood and blood products and then contaminate sterile areas.

They are not native to the western U. S. and are brought in on commerce. They normally infest apartment complexes, hospitals and large commercial buildings in this area. They rarely infest homes, but it's possible.

Harvester ants (Myrmicinae - *Pogonomyrmex* spp.)

This group of ants are commonly called "Harvester ants". They are comparatively large, 3/16" - 1/2" long, red to dark brown in color and have a pair of spines on their thorax. They have a stinger and will use it if disturbed. Harvester ants are bimorphic. They make large mounds covered in gravel, which retains heat and helps incubate the eggs in the nest below. These ants feed on seeds. They spend almost all of their time gathering food for the winter. Occasionally they are distracted such as the colony of Texas harvester ants that live in my driveway. It is impossible for me to drive into my driveway without running over their mound. For some reason which is known only to them, they refuse to move off to the side. They spend a large part of each day rebuilding the mound that was damaged by my tires. I feel sorry for them because they don't have time to forage for food and repair the damage, so I give them several handfuls of oatmeal and chicken feed every couple of days and an occasional apple muffin. The ants appear to like the offering as they gather it up quickly and take it to their storage area. While harvester ants are considered to be aggressive, in reality they are only very defensive.

During mating season, usually in late July or early August, swarmers from a harvester ant colony will fly high into the air. Most of the swarmers are males who would like to mate with the few accompanying females. Large swarms will occasionally come down chimneys or elevator shafts, much to the consternation of the inhabitants of the building. The good news is that the swarming harvester ants are not able to sting. The bad news is that there are a lot of them and they tend to congregate in large numbers and will be a nuisance. The best product to use to control harvester ants is Niban Bait, a commercial grain-like bait that is made from boric acid.

Imported fire ants (Myrmicinae - *Solenopsis invicta*)

The imported fire ants can be very dangerous. They are polymorphic and reddish-brown to black in color. They have severe stings that can cause blisters and allergic responses to the venom as well as anaphylactic shock. Over 30,000 people a year must seek medical attention in the U.S. alone from the sting of these ants.

Fire ants have successfully invaded many southern states. They have been found in Florida, Georgia, South Carolina, North Carolina, Tennessee, Alabama, Arizona, New Mexico, Mississippi, California, Louisiana, Arkansas, Texas and Oklahoma. Their mounds can be two feet in diameter and a foot and a half high. A single colony can contain close to a quarter million ants.

Fire ants will eat both plants and animals, including rodents and some reptiles. They will feed on a wide variety of plants, including strawberries, potatoes and corn. Queens in the colony will need proteins, so when you mix baits for these ants you have to make sure they are protein-based. These ants are attracted to magnetic fields and will get in transformers, air conditioners and other electrical equipment. One good thing about fire ants is that they like to feed on ticks. If you have fire ants in your yard, you won't have ticks. They will also feed on fleas, cockroaches and several species of flies.

When you control these ants, make sure you dust any electrical equipment outside with food-grade diatomaceous earth, Comet cleaner or talcum powder. This will keep the ants out of these area. For bait, you can mix boric acid or aspartame with sugar, jelly, honey or pet food. You can flood their nests with one gallon of orange juice mixed with two gallons of water and a cup of dish soap. You can also pour a couple of 2-litre bottles of Coca Cola down the mounds.

Thief ants (Myrmicinae - *Solenopsis molesta*)

Thief ants are very small ants that are related to fire ants, but resemble pharaoh ants. They are less than 1/16th of an inch long. The best way to tell them from pharaoh ants is to examine the antennae with a magnifying glass. The club on the end of the antennae has two segments in thief ants and three segments in pharaoh ants. Thief ants get their name from their habit of entering the colonies of other ant species and stealing their food.

These ants are found throughout the United States but are more common in the east and south. Outside they nest under debris on the ground or under rocks, boards or logs. In a home, they will nest in wall voids and behind baseboards.

Baits do not work well for these ants as they don't bring enough back to the colony for it to work. If you can find out where they are nesting, you can put some food-grade diatomaceous earth in the void. Cinnamon will repel them from areas you don't want them. You can also spray the ants with Greenbug for Indoors and use Greenbug for Outdoors in all the cracks and crevices around the outside of your home.

Pavement ants (Myrmicinae -*Tetramorium caespitum*)

Pavement ants are small, monomorphic, brown to black ants covered in small stiff hairs. The head and thorax are covered with small grooves that are easy to see. There are two small spines on the thorax. These ants frequently nest under concrete slabs as their name implies. They will also nest under the slab in homes and then enter the home through the expansion joints or where plumbing penetrates the slab. Once inside, they will nest inside of walls or other voids, often close to a heating source for the warmth.

They originated in Europe and are now found throughout much of the U. S., and are major pests in the northeast and midwest. They are also common in areas of California and New Mexico. They can sting and bite if disturbed. Pavement ants feed on the honeydew secretion of aphids and other insects as well as on seeds. They have very large colonies. Pavement ants readily take baits. Mix two tablespoons of peanut butter and jelly or honey with a tablespoon of boric acid or borax. If you can find their nest, you can dust it with food-grade diatomaceous earth or spray it with a cedar product such as Greenbug for Outdoors.

Argentine ants (Dolichoderinae - *Linepithema humile*)

Argentine ants are small, monomorphic and brown in color. They are one of the most successful ants species on the planet. They have huge colonies and when they move into an urban area, they displace any native ant species. Unlike other ants who fight when they encounter other colonies of their same species, Argentine ants will merge and form super-colonies, and in some cases, mega-colonies. There is one mega-colony of Argentine ants in Europe that extends over 3,700 miles and encompasses parts of Spain, Portugal, France and Italy. This mega-colony is estimated to contain hundreds of billions of ants. Argentine ants came to the United States in 1891, landing in New Orleans. Since then they have spread to several other states. They were first found in California in 1905 near Ontario. Three years later they were found in Alameda, East Oakland, San Francisco, San Jose, Los Angeles, Azusa and

Upland. The Argentine ant is now found in almost all urban areas of California where it is a major household pest. Besides California and Louisiana, there are records of these ants in Utah, New Mexico, South Dakota, Arkansas, Illinois, Florida, Alabama and Hawaii.

Outdoors I recommend using a very good cedar product called Greenbug for Outdoors. Cedar will repel most ants including Argentine ants. Spray this around your foundation every couple of days. After a couple of weeks, spray it once a week. Soon you can do it every two or three weeks. It doesn't have the residual power of a pesticide, but it isn't dangerous either. You can also use aromatic cedar mulch which will control them for several months. Also, remove all mulch (other than aromatic cedar mulch) from around the foundation of the building. Seal all cracks and crevices. Don't let any branches touch the building. If you find the nests outdoors, flood them with orange juice in soapy water.

Argentine ant workers have a sweet tooth, so indoors you can use sweet baits. Mix honey or light Karo Syrup with aspartame or 2% boric acid or borax. However, queens also have high protein requirements so you may want to make some peanut butter or fish meal baits with 2% boric acid or borax. Keep all of these baits away from children and pets.

Populations indoors are usually smaller and less active. Find the most active areas and sprinkle the areas with baking soda, Comet, Tide laundry soap, talcum powder or food grade diatomaceous earth. You should also place any of these materials in any cracks and crevices, wall voids and electrical outlets. If you see trails of ants, you can spray them with bleach or vinegar. Never spray pesticides on the ants as all you will do is kill a few and the rest will go to other areas of the house. Cedar oil repels them and the best commercial product is Greenbug for Outdoors.

Pyramid ants (Dolichoderinae - *Dorymyrmex* spp.)

Pyramid ants are reddish-brown or black and are mono-morphic. They have a distinct pyramid-shaped projection on the back of their thorax, hence their name. These small ants rarely come into homes. They usually make many small mounds around the yard and in cracks in sidewalks and on patios. They are found in most of the southern states and in California.

They will readily take a sweet bait such as jelly or honey mixed with aspartame. Terro bait is a good commercial bait. Outside, pour a cup of baking soda on the mounds, wait about a half an hour and pour a cup of vinegar on the mounds. You can also pour a 2-litre bottle of Coca Cola or Club Soda down the mound. Push a stick into the mound entrance and move it around to make the hole larger before pouring the Coca Cola or Club Soda in.

Odorous house ants (Dolichoderinae - *Tapinoma sessile*)

Odorous house ants are small, dark, reddish-brown to black ants and are monomorphic. They will follow each other in single file when entering a building. Outside they nest under objects such as rocks, boards, or any kind of debris. When they come in the home, they can nest in wall voids. If the house has a crawl space, they will nest in that area and come into the house to forage for food and water. Odorous house ants have multiple queens in a colony and hence, have large colonies.

These ants are found in all of the continental United States and adjoining parts of Canada and Mexico. They are probably the most common ant found in homes, except in areas where Argentine ants live.

They do not bite or sting. The body of the odorous house ant is relatively soft and can be easily crushed. When this occurs, a very unpleasant "coconut" odor is apparently released. I can say that in over 40 years I have never sniffed an ant so can't vouch for the smell. An average Odorous House Ant colony will have 10,000 to 40,000 members and several queens. Mating and swarming takes place in the nest and new colonies are formed by budding.

A good bait for controlling these ants indoors is two table-spoons each of peanut butter and jelly mixed with a tablespoon of boric acid or borax. A good commercial bait is Terro Ant Bait which is made from boric acid. Treat areas where they are entering your home with Greenbug for Outdoors.

Ghost ants (Dolichoderinae - *Tapinoma melanocephalum*)

Ghost ants are very small, have a black head and thorax and whitish abdomen and legs. They are monomorphic. They are common in Florida and Hawaii and are also found west to Texas. It is not known where they originated from, but they were described from Indonesia and have been found in many parts of the world, including Africa, Australia, New Zealand, Japan, and much of Polynesia.

These ants are highly adaptable and can nest outside or in your home. They may have several sub-colonies in one structure. They will nest in walls, behind cabinets, behind baseboards and in potted plants. They are very fond of green-houses. Indoors they prefer sweet foods such as syrups, sugar and cakes. Outside they will feed on dead insects and the hon-eydew secretion of aphids.

Ghost ants do not swarm. They reproduce by budding as do the pharaoh ants. Budding occurs when one or more reproductive females leave a colony with several workers and find a new location to establish a home. A good bait is two tablespoons each of peanut butter and jelly or honey mixed with one teaspoon of boric acid or borax. You can put the layer of food grade diatomaceous earth on the soil of any potted plants. When you water, it will mix in with the soil and remain effective.

White-footed ants (Dolichoderinae - *Technomyrmex difficilis*)

White-footed ants are small, black ants with white tarsi (end of legs). They are monomorphic. These ants are one of the hardest species to control. There are several reasons for this, but the primary reason is their reproductive habits seem to be designed to confuse people. Winged female white-footed ants only live a little over a year after starting a colony. When she passes on she is replaced by a wingless female who mates with a wingless male and who is capable of multiple matings. These wingless reproductive white-footed ants can comprise up to half the colony. In other words, they can reproduce faster than almost any other species of ants as they have so many queens laying eggs almost constantly. Because of their multiple queens constantly reproducing, colonies can contain up to 3 million individual ants and half of these can be reproductives. The good news is that they don't bite, sting or cause any damage. They are simply a nuisance because of their sheer numbers.

These ants are embedded in central Florida and have also been found in South Carolina, Louisiana, California and in

Montreal, Quebec, Canada.

White-footed ants feed on the nectar of some plants and the honeydew secretion of aphids and similar insects. They will actually protect these insects from their natural predators. Outdoors white-footed ants can be found under the bark of trees or even in the old galleries of termites in wooden structures. They can also live in compost piles, leaf litter, under rocks, and in outdoor furniture. They can move into homes and nest in attics, under roof shingles, in walls, and similar areas. One colony can have several branches or "satellite" colonies in or around a single home.

Yellow ants (Formicinae - *Acanthomyops* spp.)

Yellow ants are medium size ants and are yellow in color. They are monomorphic. These ants are found throughout the Midwest and New England and more commonly in the southern states including Texas and New Mexico. They feed on the honeydew secretion of aphids and similar insects. They will nest under debris on the ground around a house and in foundation walls but rarely forage in a home. Treating the areas near the foundation with Greenbug for Outdoors will help control them. If they come in the house, use a sweet bait mixed with aspartame to expel them.

Carpenter ants (Formicinae - *Camponotus* spp.)

Carpenter ants are large, polymorphic, and are black, reddish-brown, red and black or light brown in color, depending on the species. The thorax is evenly convex when viewed from the side. That differs them from field ants, who are also large but have an indented thorax. Field ants are rarely household pests.

Carpenter ants are found throughout the United States. There are a number of known species. Five species that are common include *Camponotus pennsylvanicus, Camponotus modoc, Camponotus herculeanus, Camponotus laevigatus* and *Camponotus vicinus.*

Most species are active in the late afternoons and at night. They will nest under the slabs of homes and enter through expansion joints or around plumbing. They are also found in crawl spaces under homes that have them. They will be most common in areas where there is nearby moisture. If there is damp wood available, they will make galleries to make their nests. The galleries will follow the grain of the wood. If left alone, they can hollow out and destroy structural wood. They don't eat the wood, they just carve out areas and create wood segments (frass). If they are in the house, they will forage for any foods available, including pet foods, candies, syrups, sugar and other sweet products. They will also feed on any fruits they encounter and will root through the garbage looking for grease, fat or meat scraps. You can use a bait made from two tablespoons of honey or jelly mixed with a teaspoon of boric acid and place it where the ants are foraging (keep out of the reach of children and pets). You can also put out open packets of Equal (aspartame), which they will take.

To prevent carpenter ants from entering your home, you should remove or repair all damaged wood that has a moisture problem. Make sure your gutters are clean so water doesn't back up and damage the siding or the roof and that no branches are touching the house. Store all firewood off the ground and away from the house. Remove all dead stumps and logs. I also recommend dusting your crawl space, if you have one, with food-grade diatomaceous earth. This can be done with a power duster.

If you find a nest you can spray it with a good natural pesticide, not a synthetic one that will do more harm than good.

Crazy ants (Formicinae - *Paratrechina longicornis*)

Crazy ants are black or brown, appear thin and have very long legs. They run around erratically, giving them the name. They are monomorphic. These ants are found along the coasts of California and southern Oregon in the west. They originally came from India, and can live in a variety of habitats, including areas that are very dry to areas that are wet. They will nest under wood, in tree cavities, in or under any debris left on the ground for a long time and even in potted plants. They reproduce by budding rather than by swarming.

They feed on a variety of foods, including sweets and even other insects. They particularly like house flies when they can catch them. They will also feed on the honeydew secretion from aphids and scales.

Baits should consist of sweets or proteins mixed with about 5% boric acid. They love garbage, so make sure garbage storage areas are as clean as possible. It will help to put food grade diatomaceous earth around the house under any bushes or shrubs. If you can find the nest, spray it with a good natural pesticide such as Greenbug for Outdoors.

WASPS & YELLOWJACKETS (HYMENOTPERA)

There are a number of species of wasps and yellowjackets that you may encounter, but the habits and control methods of most of them is the same. If you can't live with them in your yard, you probably should call a professional as they (wasps and yellowjackets) can be dangerous if disturbed or threatened.

Paper wasps (Vespidae; Polistinae - *Polistes* spp.)

A paper wasp queen is the lone female reproductive, who begins her nest by attaching a thick paper strand to an overhanging structure or protective site. She then builds hollow paper cells by chewing wood or plant fibers (cellulose) mixed with water and shaped with her mouthparts. There are 27 species in North America that are considered semi-social.

When a half dozen cells or so are hanging together facing downward, the Queen lays an egg near the bottom of each one. The little white grubs that hatch from the egg glue their rear ends in the cell and begin receiving nourishment in the form of chewed up bits of caterpillars provided by their mother. The fact that they feed on caterpillars makes paper wasps beneficial insects which you may want close by, but not on your house. When they grow large enough to fill the cell cavity, they break the glued spot and hold on their own by their stuffed fat bodies, hanging head down. Paper wasps are not normally aggressive until you disturb their nests. The European paper wasp is far more aggressive than our native paper wasp. This wasp first came to the United States in 1981 and has been found on both the east and west coasts and probably occurs all across the country.

From Spring on, the queen continually lays eggs and the female workers feed larvae and expand the comb or nest. Each nest can house a few to several dozen paper wasps. They do not eat the protein (insect) food they gather for the larvae but get their energy from flower nectar. Later in the season, some of the larvae develop into males and others will become next year's queens. The new males and females mate with those of other colonies, and the fertilized females find hiding places under tree bark or in logs and wait out the winter until they can begin their new colony in the spring. The male wasps die in winter; likewise the original nest disintegrates and will not be used again.

Paper wasps nests are often found near doorways and other human activity areas without occupants being stung. Colonies in trees, out-buildings, hollow fence posts and other protected places are not as easy to control as those from nests on structures.

Yellowjackets (Vespidae; Vespinae - *Vespula* spp.)

Yellowjackets are often considered serious pests that have to be eliminated from your property. If you have children playing outside or if you are allergic to stings, then they should be removed. I recommend that you hire a professional who has the proper safety equipment to deal with them as they can be dangerous.

BED BUGS (HETEROPTERA)
(Cimicidae - *Cimex lectularius*)

Bed bugs are small, nearly wingless, flattened bugs that are external parasites of humans. There are closely related species that feed on bats, cliff swallows, woodpeckers, raptors, chickens and other types of birds. Bed bugs do not transmit any diseases, but they are probably the most profitable bug in the pest control industry. If you made a list of the 100 most dangerous bugs on the planet, bed bugs wouldn't make the list. If you made a list of the top ten most profitable bugs, they would be at the top of the list. You can control bed bugs yourself in your home or business and you don't need toxic pesticides to do so.

The first step in controlling bed bugs is to completely inspect the room to determine the extent of the infestation. Pay close attention to the sleeping areas. They can be hiding anywhere but they will stay as close to the food source as possible. Small crevices in solid structures, such as the joints in the bed's headboard or between the wall and the baseboard, are the bed bugs' refuge of choice. Strip the bed so you can inspect the mattress and box spring. Examine the seams and buttons on the mattress as well as any labels. Bed bugs will hide in all of these areas. Stand the mattress on end if you have to and examine the box spring if there is one. Stand it up and look at the underside, especially along the edges. Also look behind pictures hanging on the wall, between and behind any books or magazines in close proximity to the bed and in any furniture nearby. You may have to turn some of the furniture over and examine the underside. Carefully check anything that is under the bed including storage boxes. If there is any litter under the bed, it should be removed. Also check for dried cast skins (exuviae) from the molting process and fecal matter.

Before you start the treatment, there are a few preparations you should do. Wash all the bedding in hot water (120 + degrees). This will kill any bed bugs in the bedding. Personal items such as stuffed animals, blankets, etc. should be vacuumed and placed in plastic bags for a couple of weeks. If you have a clock, phone, radio or other appliance near the bed, they should be opened and inspected as bed bugs will hide in these places as well. Thoroughly vacuum the entire room including inside closets and dresser drawers. If the infestation is severe, you will have to use a crack and crevice vacuum tool to suck the bugs out from along the edge of the carpet, from behind switch plates, from all around the bed frame, inside the box spring, and inside any furniture in the room. If you see any eggs on the mattress along the seams, you can remove these by picking them up with duct tape and discarding them or brushing them off with a stiff brush. After vacuuming the room or rooms, remove the bag from the vacuum and discard it right away.

Next, use a hair dryer to blow hot air in all the cracks and crevices and along the edge of the carpet and on the furniture to get any bed bugs the vacuuming missed. You want to get as many bed bugs as you can before the final treatment.

Now it is time to treat the bed. Use a flashlight and carefully examine the seams, buttons and any folds in the mattress along with the headboard and footboard if they are present. Check the box spring and frame as well. If you missed any bed bugs with the vacuum or hair dryer, they will be visible. Spray any bed bugs you see with the Greenbug For People (GFP) as well as all cracks and crevices in the bed. Spray the underside of the box spring as well. If you don't see any bed bugs, then spray along the seams and around the folds and all the other areas mentioned. Make sure to use plenty of solution so the sprayed surface is wet. Then put some diatomaceous earth (DE) in a duster and puff it on all the sprayed areas, including under the box spring. The GFP solution will kill any bed bugs in several hours and the DE will prevent any from hiding in these areas in the near future. You can also sprinkle fine powder body bath powder on the mattress and rub it into the fabric.

Now you have to treat all the furniture in the room including night stands, chairs, couches, dressers, etc. Make sure you carefully inspect all the wooden furniture and treat them as you treated the mattress, box spring and bed frame. If any of the furniture, such as bunk beds, have metal framing, treat inside the metal tubing with the GFP and DE.

Finally, you need to make your bed difficult for bed bugs to access. Tape up any tears in the box spring or mattress with duct tape or—better yet—enclose them in a zippered mattress cover used for dust mites. Put the legs of the bed in plastic food bowls or metal cans and coat the inside with Vaseline. Don't let the bed touch any walls or let the bed covers touch the floor.

If you have a hotel or motel, the process is the same except for the bed legs in food containers and the Vaseline. If you have or had bed bugs in your establishment, then you should treat each room as it becomes vacant. Then you can retreat them every six months or as needed.

You can trap bed bugs by placing a heating pad on the floor with sticky traps around it or you can use duct tape, sticky side up. Put an Alka-Seltzer tablet on a damp sponge on a small plate on the heating pad. The Alka-Seltzer will attract any bed bugs in the area. You can catch mosquitoes and fleas by placing two Alka-Seltzer tablets in a bowl of soapy water. Used on a damp sponge they will attract bed bugs and kissing bugs.

LICE (ANOPLURA)

Head and body lice (Pediculidae – (*Pediculus humanus*)

The three main types of lice that infest humans are the head louse, the body louse, and the crab louse. Head lice normally infest the heads of children. Children share these bugs when playing with each other at school or in other close quarters Body lice will live and breed in clothing and normally infest people who rarely change or wash their clothes. Homeless people frequently get body lice. Crab lice (Pthiridae – *Pthirus pubis*) can infest anyone as they are normally spread by sexual intercourse.

You can safely control head lice with coconut oil or olive oil shampoos or a product called Greenbug for People. Salt water will also kill lice, so if you live near an ocean, a swim would help get rid of them. You can also put a shower cap on your or your child's head and use a hair dryer. The heat from the hair dryer will kill the lice.

Body lice can be controlled by washing the person's clothing and vacuuming any beds or other furniture they may have used. Pesticides aren't necessary. Crab lice can also be controlled with coconut oil or olive oil rubbed into the area where they live. They not only live in the pubic region, but can also get in armpit hairs and the perianal region as well.

Head and body lice cannot live off the host for more than 48 hours. Crab lice are more dependent on us as they will die in 24 hours if not on their host. Head and body lice only attack humans, but crab lice aren't as fussy—they will also infest chimpanzees.

FLEAS (SIPHONAPTERA)

Cat and Dog fleas (Pulicidae - *Ctenocephalides* spp.)

There are many species of fleas throughout North America, but the ones considered pests most often are dog fleas (*Ctenocephalides canis*), and cat fleas (*Ctenocephalides felis*), as these species will infest homes. Other species carry plague and other diseases, but they will not infest a home in large numbers. Dog and cat fleas prefer parts of the country that are humid. They are not established in the arid southwest, although they occasionally turn up when brought in on a dog that moved here from somewhere else.

We have approximately 107 species of fleas in New Mexico, and about 33 species that carry the plague. Pocket gophers are known to carry seven species of fleas, but none are known to carry the plague. Pack rats can carry 34 species of fleas, and at least four are known to carry the plague. Deer mice can carry 36 species of fleas, with at least six known or suspected of carrying the plague.

The various species of squirrels can carry up to 14 species of fleas and at least eight species can carry the plague, while prairie dogs can carry 10 species of fleas. Only two species are known to be vectors of the plague and they kill the prairie dogs, so the prairie dogs can't spread the plague. In other words, if you have a colony of prairie dogs near your property, they will not spread the plague as some people falsely suggest.

Ground nesting birds such as quail and chickens can carry sticktight fleas (Echidnophaga gallinacea), and these will get on pets. They are usually found around the eyes and ears and hang on tight to your pet. I put diatomaceous earth (DE) on my fingers and rub the fleas and they will drop off. Use food-grade DE only. It is available at most feed stores.

What else can you do you do about fleas? If you have ground squirrels, I would recommend dusting the burrows with diatomaceous earth. The DE will kill any fleas in the burrow but won't hurt the squirrels. The fleas will get off the squirrel after feeding and will land in the DE in the burrow.

I never recommend using Frontline or Advantage for fleas in New Mexico. If we had dog or cat fleas, then it might be okay, but still risky. According to Whole Dog Journal, a monthly dog care and training publication, the active ingredient in Frontline, which is fipronil, may not be safe for pets.

If you have fleas infesting your home, here is what you

need to do: Steam clean the carpets. This will remove dried blood, carpet fibers and other debris, diluted excrement, some flea larvae, eggs, pupal cocoons, adults, feces and other food sources. Spray pets with a natural flea spray available at www. greenbugallnatural.com.

Put a goose-neck lamp 8" - 10" over a pan of "fizzy" seltzer water with a few drops of dish soap at night. The fleas are attracted to the heat and carbon dioxide and drown. Sprinkle salt where animals lie; salt dehydrates the fleas and they die.

To monitor infestations, slowly walk through suspected areas wearing white knee socks. When the fleas jump on you, you should clearly be able to see them on the socks. Or you can put some white pieces of fabric on the floor and the fleas will jump on them.

You can also dust the carpet with food-grade diatomaceous earth (DE). Also dust bedding, furniture and other areas your pet frequents. Let the DE sit for four days and then vacuum it up. Also rub some DE through your pet's fur to the skin, especially on the scalp and tail, behind the neck and in any area where your pet can't bite or scratch. Caution: Diatomaceous earth can dry out your pet's skin, so lightly use it no more than once a month. Borax powder used for boosting cleaning power in laundry can also be used to effectively rid your home of fleas. Borax powder is non-toxic and kills fleas by cutting into their exoskeletons. The powder can be sprinkled onto carpets and floors where flea infestations exist. Apply it to pet bedding and upholstered furniture where pets sleep, too. Work the borax powder into the surface with a stiff-bristled broom, then vacuum it up. Even though borax powder is non-toxic, use caution when young children and pets are around as it can make them sick.

FLIES (DIPTERA)

Flies are the fourth largest order of insects and there are over 100,000 species. Most of them are beneficial to some degree, as they serve as a food source to many animals and even a few plants. Many breed in organic material such as animal manure and help recycle its nutrients to the soil. Others contribute to the decomposition of dead animals. Flies can also be serious pests. Mosquitoes and other biting flies can cause human deaths by spreading such diseases as malaria, dengue fever, encephalitis, yellow fever and many others. Flies are different from other insects in that they only have a single pair of wings.

You certainly don't want flies around schools, day care centers, hospitals, nursing homes, animal shelters, or other areas where they can infect people or animals. If you have a fly problem, a good electric fly trap works well but they are expensive. I use an apple cider vinegar trap when I have issues. I monitor and identify the flies around my home with a simple fly trap, which you can easily make too. I cut the top off several plastic water bottles; invert the top into the lower portion forming a funnel. I put about two inches of apple cider vinegar in the bottle with a quarter teaspoon of sugar. Almost all flies, no matter what their normal food preference, will enter the trap. I then pour them out through a sieve, let them dry and identify them. Gallon size milk jugs cut as described above and baited with apple cider vinegar and sugar will catch a lot of flies in a large building or yard.

House flies (Muscidae - *Musca domestica*)

House flies have a gray thorax (part where head is connected and wings are attached) with four dark stripes, and a mottled abdomen (posterior portion). These flies are considered "filth flies" and will feed on excrement, garbage, carcasses, and even human secretions from wounds and mucous membranes. If you accidentally eat the larvae (maggots) in contaminated food, they can survive in your intestine. They can harbor over 100 different pathogenic organisms and are capable of transmitting more than 65 diseases and bacteria that can cause duodenal and stomach ulcers. House flies are the most common fly in the world and can be found most anywhere.

When you swat a fly remember that is has an unblurred range of vision of only about 1½ feet. You should aim your flyswatter about 1½" behind the fly, because when houseflies take off from a horizontal surface, they jump upward and backward. Set out a saucer filled with bubble soap to attract and kill flies. Adult flies eat only sugar, so mix some light Karo Syrup or honey or sugar water with 5% boric acid or borax baits.

I have frequently written about hanging Ziploc bags filled with water around doors and windows. The sun's refractive light is said to disorient flies when the sun's rays are shining through the bags and the flies won't come in the building. From the mail I've received, these bags work very well. They may not be the most attractive display, however.

Little house flies (Fannidae - *Fannia canicularia*)

Little house flies are dull gray with yellow on the upper abdomen and three dark longitudinal stripes on the top of the thorax.

These flies resemble house flies but they fly in circles in the middle of a room or on a porch and don't appear to land. They can lay their eggs in any organic material including compost piles, pet feces, dead leaves, etc. They have been known to enter the urinary tract of naked sleeping persons and causing urinary myiasis. To prevent these flies from appearing, empty and clean all food handling equipment, dishes and garbage containers and remove and/or bury animal droppings, fruit and organic debris inside and/or outside. They do like beer, so you can put two packets of aspartame in 2"of beer in an open container to act as a bait for these flies. You can also use a fly swatter with a sticky side to swat them when they are circling.

Cluster flies (Calliphoridae - *Pollenia rudis*)

Cluster flies are about ½ up to ¾ of an inch in size. Slightly larger than common house flies, they move indoors in the winter by the hundreds or even thousands of individuals, hence the name. Unlike house flies, cluster flies are not associated with poor hygiene and poor sanitary conditions. These flies do not carry diseases and other hazards that may affect humans because they do not lay their eggs in human food. They parasitize earthworms in the ground outside. When they invade homes for the winter, they will infest attics, basements, unused rooms, wall voids, ceiling voids and garages.

The best way to deal with cluster flies is to prevent them from coming in. Here are some tips: Check all the obvious entry points. Check your windows and doors for small openings. Cluster flies can squeeze through the sides of doors and windows, so make sure there isn't enough space for them to pass through. Seal or patch cracks and crevices. If you use a screen, make sure there aren't any holes that the insect can go through. Check your cellar door for possible openings too. These are entry points because your basement is an ideal undisturbed spot that cluster flies often choose to hibernate in. If you have an attic, do the same. Basically, any room or area in your home that is not visited much by any of the people in your home are the ones you should check.

Blow flies (Calliphoridae -*Phormia, Phaenicia,Cynomya* & *Calliphora*)

Blow flies are larger than house flies and are normally shiny green, blue, bronze or black in color. Blow flies feed on decaying animal matter and if you have them in your house it is an indication of a dead animal in the wall or ceiling. Occasionally the only sign of these flies in an early infestation is when the larvae fall from the ceiling onto the floor. If you can find and remove the carcass of the dead animal they are feeding on, it will speed up the process of them leaving. If you can't, there isn't much you can do except be patient and wait for the dead animal to dry up. They can also lay their eggs in dog feces or any animal matter with a high protein content, including dry cat food. Common names for the most frequently encountered blow flies are black blow flies, greenbottle flies and bluebottle flies. Greenbottle and bluebottle flies are metallic green or blue in color. Black blow flies have a black sheen. These flies are also used by forensic entomologists to establish the time of death in human fatalities.

Flesh flies (Sarcophagidae)

Flesh flies resemble house flies but differ in only having three stripes on a gray thorax. Some species lay their eggs in foul smelling dead animal matter while others will lay their eggs in open wounds on horses, cattle and other animals.

There was a case in Albuquerque several years ago where these flies laid their eggs in the festering wound of a person in a nursing home. One species can lay their eggs in the noses or eyes of humans causing myiasis, which can be serious. Proper sanitation and exclusion is the best way to control flesh flies.

Fruit flies (Drosophilidae)

Fruit flies are usually found in the kitchen where they feed and breed on food spilled in out of the way places such as behind or under appliances or similar areas. These small flies have distinctive red eyes, which you can see with a hand lens. They are tan or brown in color and about 1/8" long. They are also known as pomace flies and vinegar flies. They can be serious pests when found in food handling establishments as they breed in and feed on fruits, vegetables and any moist, decaying organic material. They have been known to cause intestinal problems and diarrhea when fruit containing their larvae are eaten. They will also breed in discarded fruit juice and soft drink cans and in unsecured bottles of wine. They are also very prolific as the female can lay about 500 eggs which will hatch and reach adulthood in as little as eight days.

These little flies can be beneficial, though, as they have been studied in research on genetics. The species *Drosophila melanogaster* is most-often used in genetic and heredity studies, and is also a very common fly in many homes and businesses.

You can control fruit flies in your home by totally eliminating all breeding material. They are attracted to acetic acid (vinegar), so put some drops on duct tape or glue boards; or, just fill a small paper cup with vinegar and the flies will dive right in.

Hump-backed flies (Phoridae)

Phorids are small flies, about an 1/8" long and tan to dark brown in color. They have a distinct hump-backed shape thorax, hence their common name. They do not have red eyes as fruit flies do. When these flies are disturbed, they will run along the surface they are on rather than flying away.

These flies breed in any moist organic material including dirty mops, garbage, decaying fruits and vegetables and dead animal matter. They are also known as coffin flies because of their presence where dead bodies are found, including the inside of coffins. There are over 220 species of phorid flies in the United States.

You have to eliminate the food source and breeding areas in order to control them in your home or business.

Dung flies (Sphaeroceridae)

Sphaerocerid flies are sometimes called dung flies, but that name probably isn't appropriate. While they will breed in dung, they will also breed in other organic materials and are often found in areas where phorid or drosophilid flies breed. Sphaerocerids can be recognized by the enlarged size of the first tarsal segment on their hind legs. The tarsi are the last five segments on the leg. They are very small, about an 1/8 of an inch and dark-colored. There are over 240 species of sphaerocerids in the United States, and they are easily transported around the country as they breed in decaying material carried in commerce between states.

These flies will breed in cracks in the floor, unclean trash containers and even the bottom of elevator shafts if it is damp and has matter there. They can be a problem in food establishments if there is a lot of spilled food that works its way into floor cracks or expansion joints. The best way to control these flies is to find our where they are breeding and totally eliminate the rotting material from the area.

Moth flies (Psychodidae)

Moth flies are small flies with hairy wings that resemble small moths. They are also called filter flies and drain flies. They are usually found in the bathroom. They will breed in the gunk buildup in drains and will often be found in the tub, on shower curtains or the wall. They are poor fliers and seem to just hop around. The larvae live in gelatinous material in sink and floor drain traps, in sewer treatment plants and in septic tanks. They will also breed in damp crawl spaces under a house. In a commercial building you can put duct tape sticky side down on drains to see which ones they are breeding in. You need to keep your drains clean to control these flies as they have a very short life cycle. They can go from egg to adult in a little over a week in some areas.

Fungus Gnats (Sciaridae)

Fungus gnats are very small flies with long legs and long antennae and distinctly patterned wings. They are dark brown or black in color. They are generally found in over-watered house plants where the larvae feed on fungus in the potting soil and moist organic material. The best way to control them is to let the plants dry out almost to the point of wilting before re-watering. That will kill the larvae in the soil. Then put an inch of aquarium gravel on the soil to prevent female fungus gnats from laying any more eggs in the potting soil. You can also place a yellow sticky trap on a stick in the soil to catch the adult gnats.

Mosquitoes (Culicidae)

Mosquitoes are small, slender, biting flies. They have a long, thin mouth designed for piercing the skin and sucking out blood. They require water to lay their eggs. They are very important disease vectors and can transmit West Nile Virus, Encephalitis and other diseases in the United States. If you have mosquitoes, make sure you wear a good non-DEET mosquito repellent when you go outside. Never use the DEET products that government agencies recommend as DEET (N,N-diethyl-m-toluamine) is a chemical that some people have severe reactions to. It is a fact that DEET works well as long as it is full strength.

However, when it begins to weaken, it actually attracts mosquitoes and you have to put more on, which means absorbing more of the chemicals into your system. Most non-DEET products (catnip, citronella, and lemongrass) are effective for two or three hours before having to be reapplied, but they do not contain potentially dangerous chemicals.

Remove all standing or stagnant water if at all possible. This means old tires, barrels, cans, wading pools, bird baths, and other items that can hold water. You can apply a light coating of food-grade diatomaceous earth on any water that can't be removed. Eucalyptus oils, garlic extracts and extracts of orange and lemon peels will kill mosquito larvae in the water.

If you have adult mosquitoes in your grass or bushes, you can spray them with Greenbug for Outdoors. Catnip is a very good repellent according to a report from Iowa State University. Other good repellents include lemongrass, basil, birch, mint, rosemary, spearmint and yarrow. Geraniums or basil plants planted near your doors will repel mosquitoes. Citronella and pennyroyal both work but have side affects. Pennyroyal may increase the risk of a miscarriage for pregnant women, and citronella has been known to attract female black bears. Test anything you put on your skin on a small portion first to make sure you aren't allergic to it.

Again, I cannot stress enough, never use repellents that contain DEET.

MOTHS (LEPIDOPTERA)

There are several types of moths that can become household pests. Clothes moths can damage clothing and pantry moths can infest some stored foods. Other moths that come in the house are occasional invaders and won't do any damage. I recommend gently catching them and putting them outside.

Clothes moths (Tineidae)

There are two distinct types of clothes moths commonly found in homes. They are both small moths. The webbing clothes moth (*Tineola bisselliella*) is a solid golden brown on the wings, while the casemaking clothes moth (*Tinea pellionella*) has three black spots on each wing. Casemaking clothes moth larvae construct a small bag from material to protect their body from the environment. They drag the bag or tube wherever they feed.

Clothes moths are occasionally found in closets where they lay their eggs on suitable fabric. The larvae hatch and feed on the fabric doing damage. There are several things you can do to prevent clothes moths. First, keep clothes and other fabrics stored in sealed, plastic bags. Next you can hang some repellents in the closets. Put dried lemon peels, cedar chips, dried rosemary or mint in cheese cloth bags and hang them in the closets. Make sure any carpets in the closet are clean and free of lint or animal hair or any organic debris.

If you already have webbing clothes moths, you should hang one Clothes Moth Pheromone Trap in each closet. It will attract and catch the male moths and stop the breeding process. Don't hang more than one trap or you will confuse the moths and they will just fly around, not sure where to go. The pheromone traps aren't effective against casemaking clothes moths. Dry cleaning all the clothes will kill all the stages of the moths as well as washing all infested clothing in hot, soapy water to kill the larvae and eggs.

Indian meal moths (Pyralidae - *Plodia interpunctella*)

There are several species of pantry moths that can infest your home, but the one most frequently encountered is the Indian meal moth. This moth is small and colorful. The wings are gray toward the body and have dark bands near the tip.

They will feed on a wide variety of dried foods, including cereals, flour, cornmeal, crackers, cake mixes, pasta, dried pet foods, candy, powdered milk, chocolate candy and many other foodstuffs.

The best control is to hang one Flour Moth Pheromone Trap in the area they are infesting. This will attract and catch the male moths and stop the breeding process. Then inspect all open dried foods and toss anything that is infested. Place all non-infested foods in sealed containers or refrigerate them. Completely clean the pantry where the foods are stored to get any larvae that may be crawling around. Then lightly dust the shelves with food-grade diatomaceous earth before putting the foods back.

BEETLES (COLEOPTERA)

There are three groups of beetles that can cause problems in a home. Carpet beetles will damage carpets, clothing, animal fur, feathers, and similar products. Stored product beetles will infest many dried foods and wood boring beetles can damage the structure of a home or wooden objects in it.

Carpet Beetles (Dermestidae)

Carpet beetle larvae are small, about 1/4" long and carrot-shaped with long hairs. They will feed on anything organic. The adult beetles are small, round and usually black in color, sometimes with lighter markings.

The best method for controlling carpet beetles is by completely cleaning everything. Steam clean the carpets if possible as well as any upholstered furniture. Make sure you vacuum under all furniture as carpet beetles can survive feeding on dust bunnies. Keep a bottle of Greenbug for Indoors available to directly spray and adults or larvae you find. Make sure you vacuum up all the dead insects as the spines on the carpet beetle larvae can cause rash problems if they penetrate your pores.

Also, adult carpet beetles feed on the nectar in flowers so they don't do any damage beyond breeding indoors. If you have flowers blooming near your house, you will attract adult carpet beetles. Make sure there aren't ways for them to get into your home.

Flour beetles (Tenebrionidae – *Tribolium* spp.)

Flour beetles are small, brownish in color and elongate in shape. There are nine species that are potential pests in stored food products. Two species are very common. The confused flour beetle (*Tribolium confusum*) is common in northern regions and the red flour beetle (*Tribolium castaneum*) is more common in southern areas. They feed on barley, beet pulp, breakfast cereals, grains, nuts, wheat, wheat bran, milk chocolate, dried milk and occasionally hides. Good sanitation is key to controlling these beetles. Freezing stored products at -4 degrees for 24 hours will kill all stages, as will heating at 122 degrees for an hour.

Drugstore beetles (Anobiidae – *Stegobium paniceum*)

These beetles have a hood-like thorax which hides the head when viewed from above. They are reddish brown in color and rounded in profile and oval-shaped. They feed on a variety of products including tobacco, seeds, grain, nuts, beans, spices, dried fruits and vegetables, flour, rice, ginger, yeast, herbs, paprika, dry dog and cat food, cocoa, biscuits, raisins, dates, alfalfa, hay, almond hulls, barley, corn meal, rice meal, wheat bran and even rodenticides. They are good at penetrating packaging to get access to food. The same control methods recommended for flour beetles will work on this species.

Saw-toothed grain beetles (Silvanidae – *Oryzaephilus surinamensis*)

Saw-toothed grain beetles are small, black, elongate and have six distinct saw-like teeth on each side of the thorax. They are commonly associated with breakfast cereals and are frequently found in corn meal, flour, biscuit mix, and processed cereals, as well as in alfalfa seed, almonds, baking soda, barley, candy, clover seeds, chocolate, sugar, rice, wheat, cereals, dried fruits, corn, cornmeal, corn starch, flour, garbanzos, hay, honeycomb, milo, mixed feeds, oats, raisins, rice, figs, peas, pecans, dried meat and tobacco. Sanitation and freezing and heating also works on these beetles.

Hide & Larder beetles (Dermestidae – *Dermestes* spp.)

Dermestid beetles are larger than other stored product beetles, reaching a 1/3 of an inch long. The hide beetle is brown on top and white on the bottom and the larder beetle is brown with a broad cream-colored band across the front of the abdomen. These beetles prefer animal products such as leather goods, hides, skins, dried fish, pet food, bacon, cheese and feathers. They can be a major pest in museums. Sanitation is important and sticky traps can be used on flat surfaces to catch adult and larval dermestid beetles.

Weevils (Curculionidae – *Sitophilus* spp.)

Weevils are easily recognized by their small size and prominent snout. They are very destructive towards stored grains in our world. They will feed on chickpeas, corn, oats, barley, rye, wheat, kafir, buckwheat and millet. They are frequently found in macaroni and noodles. When you find any of these beetles in your home, inspect all open dried foods and toss anything that is infested. Place all non-infested foods in sealed containers or refrigerate them. Completely clean the pantry where the foods are stored to get any larvae that may be crawling around.

Then lightly dust the shelves with food-grade diatomaceous earth before putting the foods back.

False powder post beetles (Anobiidae & Bostrichidae)

There are a number of species of beetles in this family that attack wood. They will attack new and old hardwoods and soft-woods with a 12% moisture content. They are recognized by their hood-like thorax that hides the head when viewed from above. They have a cylindrical body shape and are reddish-brown to brownish-black in color. They are often found infesting wood joists and sill plates in crawl spaces under homes. Two common species are the deathwatch beetle (*Xestobium rufovillosum*), the furniture beetle (*Anobium punctatum*). The furniture beetle will infest furniture and pine flooring.

Other beetles in these two families include the California deathwatch beetle (*Hadrobregmus gibbicollis*) which occurs along the Pacific Coast. *Xyletinus pelatus* (no common name) is found in the eastern United States and attacks cellar joists and flooring in damp buildings. *Nicobium castaenum* (no common name) is found in Virginia and South Carolina to Louisiana, and attacks furniture and pine woodwork. The lead cable borer (*Scobicia declivis*) normally infests dead and seasoning oak and damage can be severe. It is found throughout the west and is most common in California.

The best method of control for all wood-boring beetles is to treat all exposed wood with a sodium borate, which will prevent them from reinfesting the wood after they emerge.

Powder post beetles (Bostrichinae; Lyctinae – *Lyctus* spp.)

Powder post beetles are small, elongate and almost always

infest hardwoods. They frequently infest lumber, woodwork, furniture, tool handles, gun stocks and similar items. They produce very fine, powder-like frass when they damage wood. Frass from anobiids and bostrichids is not nearly as fine as these beetles produce. They are second only to termites in destructive capability. There are several destructive species nationwide. The brown powder-post beetle (*Lyctus brunneus*) is found in most states and is frequently found infesting imported hardwood products. The western powder-post beetle (*Lyctus cavicollis*) is found throughout the United States and attacks oak firewood and hickory, orange and eucalyptus wood. The European powder-post beetle (*Lyctus linearis*) is found in the eastern United States and attacks hickory, oak, ash, walnut and wild cherry wood. The southern powder-post beetle (*Lyctus planicollis*) is found nationwide but does most of its damage in the southern states. It prefers seasoned or partially seasoned wood of oak, ash and hickory. The white-marked powder-post beetle (*Trogoxylon parallelopipedum*) is a common native species and has the same food preferences the southern powder-post beetle.

Long-horned borers (Cerambycidae)

Only a few species of long-horned beetles are pests of wood in homes. The old house borer (*Hylotrupes bajulus*) is probably the most destructive species in this family of beetles. It is found from Maine to Florida and west to Michigan to Texas. There have been some reports of this beetle in California. They are between ½ and ¾ inches long and are slightly flattened. They are brownish-black in color. Each wing cover has a gray band on it.

They are usually built into a house with wood from storage as adults have been found at lumber mills in seasoned and unseasoned wood. The frass is slightly granular and composed of small, barrel-shaped pellets of digested wood and irregular shaped wood fragments that were not eaten. The larvae can feed on the wood from 2 to 10 years before maturing into adulthood, depending on environmental conditions.

Metallic wood borers (Buprestidae)

The larval form of these beetles are called flat-headed borers, because the exit holes in the wood are oval, not round as in most other wood boring beetle larvae. Only a few species will attack seasoned wood, so they aren't a serious pest. The adult beetles are often brightly colored and metallic. They are boat shaped in appearance. The most destructive species is the golden metallic borer (*Buprestis aurulenta*). The wings are greenish-blue with copper margins. They will attack flooring and woodwork of Douglas fir that isn't finished with paint or varnish. They also feed on pine and spruce lumber. These beetles are found throughout the western United States.

TERMITES (ISOPTERA)

There are close to 2500 species of termites described worldwide. If you weighed all of the termites, they would weigh twice as much as all of the humans on the planet. There are over 50 species in the United States, but only a few species of subterranean termites and drywood termites are serious pests.

Drywood termites (Kalotermidae – *Incisitermes* spp.)

Drywood termites do not need soil contact. They live in

dry, sound wood, usually near the surface. They get what moisture they require from the wood they feed on and from the water formed during digestion of that wood. Drywood swarmers generally enter your home at night through unscreened attic or foundation vents or through cracks and crevices between exposed wood. Drywood termites are most commonly recognized by their distinctive fecal pellets (piles) that are often the color of the wood they are feeding upon. The fecal pellets are kicked out of the wood by the nymphs (workers) through "kick holes" that are visible. *Incisitermes minor* is found in much of California where it is a major pest. It is also found in Arizona, Utah, and New Mexico. *Incisitermes snyderi, Incisitermes schwarzi* and *Kalotermes approximatus* are species found in the southeastern states that are of economic importance because of the damage they can do.

The best method of control from a professional standpoint is the use of XT-2000 Orange oil. If you live in north-central California, Planet Orange is the best termite control company in the area. If you have a localized infestation that you can reach, then you can inject some Greenbug for Indoors into the kickout holes in the wood. You can also do this with furniture infested by drywood termites.

Subterranean termites (Rhinotermitidae)

Subterranean termites are social insects with very large colonies. They consist of a queen, sexual reproductives, workers and soldiers. The workers are grayish or white and wingless. They are the ones in the colony that forage for food. They also groom the queens, eggs, nymphs and soldiers, and build the nest. Workers are the ones who do the damage to the wood. The workers have a mass of unique genera and species of oxymonad, trichomonad, and hypermastigote flagellates (protozoa) in their lower digestive tract and it is these protozoans that enable the termites to digest wood. When the protozoans are killed, the termites will quickly starve and the entire colony will die off as the workers feed the other caste members in the colony through a process call trophallaxis. Trophallaxis is food sharing between members of the same colony and is what makes products such as antibiotics and borates so effective. Tetracycline is an anti-biotic and effectively kills the protozoans in the termites digestive system and will reduce the colony or eliminate it if it isn't too large.

Western subterranean termites (*Reticulitermes hesperus*)

This is the western subterranean termite. It is found from British Colombia south to western Mexico and is very common along the Pacific coastal areas. It occurs as far east as Idaho and Nevada. Their colonies can reach several hundred thousand individuals and the colony has to be about three years old before they can swarm. They do extensive damage and will attack fence posts, utility poles, any wood products on the ground, and living plants and trees.

Eastern subterranean termites (*Reticulitermes flavipes*)

The eastern subterranean termite is the most destructive species in this group. It is found throughout the eastern United States and as far west as eastern New Mexico. It occurs in spotty areas of Utah and Arizona as well. They have very large colonies, numbering as many as ¼ million individuals. They go below the frost line during extremely cold weather, and build earth-like shelter tubes over obstacles like the desert subterranean termite.

Arid land subterranean termites (*Reticulitermes tibialis*)

This is the arid land subterranean termite. It is found in arid desert areas and higher elevations and ranges from Oregon and Montana south to Mexico and eastward to Missouri, Arkansas and Texas. This is the most common termite in New Mexico. It is the least destructive of the termites in this group, although it can still cause considerable damage in some situations.

Desert subterranean termites (*Heterotermes aureus*)

This is the desert subterranean termite. It is found in desert regions of southern Arizona and California. It is common in the Phoenix area but not as common near Tucson. This termite is very destructive. It will attack sound dry wood, utility poles and posts. It will build earth-like tube shelters over obstacles to get to edible wood. The western subterranean and arid land termites do not build these tube-like shelters.

Formosan subterranean termites (*Coptotermes formosanus*)

Formosan termites are larger than our native subterranean termites. They were introduced from Asia by stowing away on ships. They are very destructive and attack all kinds of wood and cellulose products. They will also attack living plants when moisture is not available elsewhere. They have been known to hollow a building wall in three months in Hawaii. They can also attack and become established on wooden ship hulls and in this way, be transported from port to port. Evidence of their presence is found in channels between pieces of wood. Passageways or dirt-colored tubes are usually built on foundations. They do not have to maintain ground contact if adequate moisture is available, so a normal subterranean treatment may not be effective. Colonies are large and contain several hundred thousand individuals.

Formosan termites are established in Hawaii and have been introduced in Texas, Louisiana, and South Carolina. Isolated cases have been found in California.

Subterranean Termite Control

Over a half million homes are treated every year with toxic pesticides to control these insects. In nature, they are beneficial insects as they break down dead wood and consume it. If it weren't for termites there would be a whole lot more dead trees laying around. Unfortunately, termites can't differentiate a dead tree from the wood in your house. It's all edible to them.

There are several products I recommend for controlling termites. They are sodium borates (TimBor and BoraCare are two brand names), Tetracycline (Terramycin, Sumycin, Tetracyn, Panmycin and Duramycin are brand names) and food-grade diatomaceous earth. Colloidal silver, diluted boric acid or borax and aspartame can also be used.

Sodium borates are registered termiticides / insecticides that are safe to use. They will permanently penetrate wood and make it totally inedible for any wood-eating insect. In New Zealand they have required all wood that is put into homes be treated with a sodium borate before being installed. They put this requirement into place in 1953, and they don't have a termite industry as termites are never found in their homes. Sodium borates are also effective wood fungi decay preventatives and fire retardants. They should be applied to all exposed wood, especially in a crawl space, and are safe as they easily wash off and there is no risk of absorption through unbroken skin.

Termites will not only die if they feed on wood treated with sodium borates, but they will be killed for just crawling over it. If adult beetles emerge from wood treated with a sodium borate, they will not die, but they will be prevented from re-infesting the wood. BoraCare is a liquid sodium borate and TimBor is a wettable powder. BoraCare would probably be easier for the homeowner to use. BoraCare and TimBor are not available in stores. You can get them online from suppliers such as www.pestcontrolsupplies.com. Tetracyclines are often given to livestock to control and treat bacterial infections. You can buy tetracycline at most feed stores.

While a professional termite treatment by a reputable company is recommended, particularly if you are buying or selling a home, it is entirely possible to treat your home yourself without using a pest control company or toxic pesticides. Termidor is a very good termiticide and relatively "safe" as pesticides go. It is also a General Use pesticide so can be used by anyone. (Restricted Use pesticides can only be used by certified professionals.) You can get Termidor online if you want to use it, from www.pestcontrolsupplies.com or other similar sites. This method works best if you live in an area where you have arid land subterranean termites as they are not as voracious and you can eliminate them with a spot treatment. If you are dealing with any of the other species, you are probably better off using a professional. When doing it yourself, you will need to drill a couple of holes in the slab near where the infestation is. Then mix some Termidor according to the label and inject it into the holes, and spray some Termidor foam where you see the evidence. This method will work on arid land termites, which are common in New Mexico, parts of Arizona, Utah and Nevada and some other areas. Make sure this is the species in your home before going this route.

If you have eastern, western or desert subs, you can monitor them around your home, and possibly wipe out a colony, using tetracycline. Tetracyclines are often given to livestock to control and treat bacterial infections, and can be bought at most feed stores. Termite workers have intestinal microorganisms containing protozoans in their lower digestive system and these microorganisms contain enzymes that help them digest cellulose. The Tetracycline will kill the protozoans and prevent the termites from being able to digest the cellulose which will kill the entire termite colony. I recommend adding boric acid or borax to the solution to make it work even faster.

Here is what you need to get started. Dig several shallow holes (about 4"-6") in the ground about a foot from your foundation. If you have rocks or mulch around the house you will have to move some of it so you can dig. If you have concrete sidewalks all around your house, you will have to dig next to them, although that may slow the termite eradication process down a little.

Then get some flat pieces of cardboard, some paper towels, or even a few paper plates. I have used all three and each works. I dilute a packet of tetracycline, mixed with three tablespoons of boric acid and a half gallon of water. I soak the paper towels/paper plates or the cardboard and then put them in the holes and cover them. Place these bait stations around the house, one in each corner and one in between each corner about a foot from the foundation.

Check the bait stations about 10 days after putting them in the ground. If you find over 100 worker termites and a dozen or so soldiers, it means the entire colony is involved and will soon be eliminated. This would be a good time to put fresh cardboard/paper towels soaked with tetracycline and boric acid or borax in the ground. Then check the stations bi-weekly and replace accordingly if you see continued activity.

If you have a crawl space under your home, place the cardboard/paper towel/paper plates bait stations in several areas under the house where it is accessible to you. Then, to prevent any termite activity in the future, you can treat along the bottom of the inside foundation wall with diatomaceous earth, borax, or salt. Termites will avoid all of these products. They may live in the soil but they won't climb the foundation to get to the wooden sub-floor. Make sure you treat around any support piers as well. Then treat all the exposed wood with a sodium borate (TimBor or BoraCare). That will not only protect the sub-floor from termites but will also prevent woodboring beetles from infesting the wood. Finally, get a power duster and blow several pounds of food-grade diatomaceous earth under the house on the bare soil. This will prevent termites from building mud tubes out of the ground and into the wood. It will also deter other insects and spiders from living in the crawl space.

If you are building a home and want to treat the soil without using pesticides, you can do it with natural products. You can apply a generous amount of food-grade diatomaceous earth on the ground before the vapor barrier is put down. Put a lot around the outside of the footing and around where the pipes will penetrate the slab. Termites will not travel through soil treated with diatomaceous earth.

SCORPIONS (SCORPIONES) AND
CENTIPEDES (CHILOPODA)

Scorpions and centipedes are two groups of arthropods that nobody wants in their homes. Both of these animals have the capability of stinging (scorpions) you or biting (centipedes) you with painful results. Only one species of scorpion in this country is dangerously venomous. It is the bark scorpion (*Centruroides sculpturatus*), found in Arizona and southwestern New Mexico. The bark scorpion has killed a few people in Arizona, but not in the last 40 years. Centipede bites are painful, but not deadly in this country. There *are* some very large centipedes in Asia that have caused human fatalities, but none in the United States. However, that being said, anyone can be allergic to anything, including the bite or sting of an insect or some other arthropod. Even if the bites or stings aren't fatal, they can certainly be painful.

There are over two hundred species of centipedes in the western U. S., but most of them are very small and belong to two suborders. These are the stone centipedes (Lithobiomorpha) and the soil centipedes (Geophilomorpha). Stone centipedes are about an inch long and have 15 pair of legs. Soil centipedes aren't much longer and have upwards of 40 pair of legs; neither group is capable of biting people. Both are common in yards and feed on small bugs, so they can be considered beneficial.

House centipedes (*Scutigera coleoptrata*) are about an inch long and have 15 pair of very long legs. They are common almost everywhere and are often found in homes. They rarely bite, and feed on such pests as spiders, bed bugs, termites, cockroaches, ants and silverfish, so they should probably be welcome in the home.

Three species of Scolopendromorpha centipedes are found in the western states. The desert centipede (*Scolopendra polymorpha*) is most common throughout the west with the exception of Washington. It is about three or four inches long. The green centipede (*Scolopendra viridis*) is found in the mountainous areas of New Mexico, Arizona, southeastern Colorado, Utah and extreme southern Nevada. It is only a couple of inches long. The giant desert centipede (*Scolopendra heros*) is found in the southern and eastern portions of New Mexico, much of Arizona, and the extreme southeast portion of Colorado. This species can reach a length of 6.5 inches and is capable of killing and eating mice. All of the *Scolopendra* have painful bites but they are not dangerous.

Centipedes and scorpions are usually found in areas of high moisture such as in loose bark or rotting logs, and under stones, boards, railroad ties, trash, piles of leaves, and grass clippings. They are nocturnal—active at night—and hide by day in the earth, crawling out at night to hunt. They occasionally invade structures and will feed on cockroaches, crickets, spiders, etc. Although they may be found anywhere in a building, including beds, the usual places are damp basements, bathrooms, and any crawl space under the home or building.

Keeping them out of structures is most important, and this begins with ensuring that no tree or shrub branches are touching the structure. Branches can be pruned back to eliminate this common pathway. You also can carefully examine the entire exterior—including up to the eaves—as scorpions and other pests may crawl up rough surfaces. You want to permanently fill in any openings found and ensure all vent screens are in place and in good condition. In the yard you can eliminate many potential harborage sites for scorpions and centipedes such as rocks, boards, and other objects resting on the soil. Scorpions will also hide under bark on trees, so dust these with food grade diatomaceous earth where loose bark is found.

Firewood should be stacked on racks off the soil and kept outside until immediately ready to burn. Garbage cans should be elevated. Keep grass mowed to prevent hiding areas for scorpions, centipedes, and other pests. and weeds should be eliminated.

If you find a scorpion or centipede in your home, spray it with some Greenbug for Indoors. Don't use synthetic pesticides as they are more dangerous than the scorpion or centipede.

SPIDERS (ARACHNIDA)

Although most spiders possess venom glands, most are too small to break the skin with their fangs and have no desire to do so. All spiders will bite in self defense if they are handled carelessly or squeezed. Most bites occur when people roll over in bed or when they put on their clothes and a spider is inside the clothing.

I am certainly not saying all spiders are harmless. Black widows are capable of producing a serious bite, and any such bite by this spider should be considered a major medical emergency. The brown recluse is also dangerously venomous. Sac spiders and wolf spiders can give serious, though not fatal, bites, particularly if you are allergic to any of the components of the venom. Daddy longlegs (aka harvestmen) are not at all dangerous despite their reputation to the contrary. Jumping spiders are interesting to watch but are not dangerous although a large one can bite if mishandled. Most of the small hunting spiders such as ground spiders are incapable of hurting anyone.

To control spiders around your home if you don't want them, here are a few suggestions. Control the lighting at night that attracts their food, flying insects. Keep trash and rubbish out of your yard. If you have firewood, stack it somewhere where there is a lot of sunlight and cover it with black plastic. It will get so hot under there that spiders and other insects/arachnids won't go in the wood. Seal any cracks or crevices around the house that would let hunting spiders inside. If your doors do not close tightly, install door sweeps on them.

Make sure your bed isn't touching the wall. This will make it harder for spiders to get into bed with you. Don't leave clothing on the floor. If you do, completely shake it out before putting it on. If you must kill spiders instead of releasing them outside, use a natural product like Greenbug for Indoors.

Black widow spiders (Theridiidae – *Latrodectus* spp.)

There are three main species in the black widow group. The eastern black widow (*Latrodectus mactans*), the western black widow (*Latrodectus hesperus*), and the brown widow (*Latrodectus geometricus*). The eastern black widow is found throughout the east with the exception of Maine, New Hampshire, and most of Vermont. The western black widow is found in every state west of central North Dakota and south to Texas. The brown widow is found in Florida and Texas and may be expanding into neighboring states. All the female widow spiders have a reddish hourglass-shaped marking on the underside of a shiny black abdomen. The abdomen is brown in the brown widow.

Medical: The black widow is feared everywhere although it isn't as dangerous as we are told. The toxic venom is neurotoxic, but the spider injects very little material and the death rate is about 1%. Additionally, the black widow is not inclined to bite unless it is squeezed or defending its egg sac in a web. I pick them up all the time and have never had one try to bite me.

False black widows (Theridiidae – *Steatoda grossa*)

The false black widow is often mistaken for the real black widow. They are about the same size and the same color. The false black widow does not have the red hourglass marking on its abdomen. It usually has a yellowish band across the front portion of its abdomen on top. It originally came from Europe and is found along both coasts, the states that border the Great Lakes, in Colorado, Arizona and New Mexico, as well as in a few other inland states. It is absolutely harmless and like the real black widow, it is very timid and non-aggressive.

Recluse spiders (Sicariidae – *Loxosceles* spp.)

The brown recluse spider (*Loxosceles reclusa*) is shy, sedentary, and builds an irregular web that is often not even recognized as a spiderweb. It has a fiddle-shaped pattern on its cephalothorax. Females lay eggs in flattened egg sacs that are frequently attached to the underside of objects. When they are indoors, they can usually be found in dark places, beneath or behind furniture, in boxes or storage areas, among stored books and papers, and similar areas. Outside they live under rocks, boards and other dark areas.

The brown recluse is found from eastern areas of the

country west to Texas, Oklahoma, and eastern New Mexico. It is frequently transported to different areas of the country in luggage or by commercial vehicles. There are several other species of *Loxosceles* in the southwestern states. None of them have bitten anyone so we don't know if they are potentially dangerous or not. One species introduced into California and Massachusetts, *Loxosceles laeta*, is potentially dangerous. It occasionally comes to the United States in products shipped from South America.

Medical: Brown Recluse bites are not painful at the time of the bite. About an hour or so afterward there may be intense pain at the site where bitten. There is usually a dark depressed area at the site of the bite, which will turn darker in a day or so. The dead tissue will slough away and the bite area will scar over. Death seldom if ever occurs, but the bite is extremely debilitating and traumatic. If you know you were bitten by a brown recluse, seek medical attention right away.

Hobo spiders (Agelenidae – *Tegenaria agrestis*)

The Hobo Spiders or the aggressive house spiders are in the genus *Tegenaria*. Since 1982, many brown recluse spider bites in the Northwest were shown to actually be hobo spider bites. *Tegenaria agrestis* was first introduced into the ports of Seattle in the late 1920s and has been moving south ever since. It is now found in Washington, Oregon, Idaho, western Montana, and much of Utah. They originally came from Europe where they are most commonly found inside homes. Generally, these spiders are yellow to pale tan in color with long legs. These spiders occur in the highest frequency in July through September when they are reproducing. Females produce an egg sac that is placed near the opening of the funnel in their webs.

Medical: Although the bite of these species is not considered to be as dangerous as that of either the brown recluse or widow spiders, it can cause a similar ulceration or lesions of the skin as the brown recluse and may involve systemic reactions. The venom is a necrotic type that can cause tissue death and sloughing of the skin next to the bite. The wound can require up to 6 months to heal. Dogs and cats are also bitten, with some deaths occurring.

Common house spiders (Agelenidae – *Tegenaria domestica*)

This may be one of the most common spiders found in homes in the country. It is found in every state, most Canadian provinces, and virtually all over the world. The cephalothorax (section where legs are attached) is shiny brown with two longitudinal stripes running down the middle. The abdomen is grayish with a series of chevron shaped markings running down the middle to the end. The legs are brownish-gray with black bands. The similar and more aggressive hobo spider does not have bands on the leg. The common house spider is harmless and feeds on a lot of household pest insects, so it can be considered beneficial.

Orb-weaver spiders (Araneidae)

Orb-weavers (family Araneidae) are large spiders that make distinct orb-like webs that are often very close to or attached to homes. The pumpkin spider, which is large, has two humps and a distinct pattern that often scares people; however, it is common in many areas and is absolutely harmless.

Ground spiders (Gnaphosidae)

Ground spiders (family Gnaphosidae) are very common and are frequently found indoors. They live under debris on the ground outside and often wander into homes. Most of them are completely harmless. One species, the eastern parson spider (*Herpyllus ecclesiasticus*), can give a painful, but not a dangerous bite. However, some people do suffer allergic reactions to the bite, like any other insect bite, so it's something to be aware of. This spider is about 1/2" long, and is blackish with a distinctive white or pink pattern on the middle of it's back. The marking resembles an old-style cravat worn by clergy in the 18th century. This spider is found almost everywhere east of the Rocky Mountains. A very similar species, the western parson spider (*Herpyllus propinquus*) is found west of the mountains.

Sac Spiders (Clubionidae – *Cheiracanthium* spp.)

Sac spiders are responsible for spider bites in homes more often than most other species. They have a cytotoxic venom, which is the same as the brown recluse, although it isn't as toxic. It is possible many sac spider bites are blamed on the recluse. Two species are referred to as yellow sac spiders due to their similar coloration. They are *Cheiracanthium inclusum* and *C. mildei*. They are light yellowish to a pale yellowish-green, sometimes with a orange-brown stripe on top of the abdomen. They are small, 1/4"-3/8" long. Yellow sac spiders are found throughout the country.

Female sac spiders build a silken tube or sac in a protected area, often under furniture. They usually come out at night to hunt and that is when most bites take place. Often the bite results in a sharp pain, but some people won't feel anything.

Jumping spiders (Salticidae)

Jumping spiders are easily distinguished from other spiders by their four big eyes on the face and four smaller eyes on top of the head. Around the world there are probably more than 5,000 species of jumping spiders. In the U. S. there are at least 40 genera and more than 300 species.

Jumping spiders are charming spiders that look up and watch you. Their excellent vision allows them to hunt and spot their prey from long distances, creeping up then pouncing using their jumping ability.

The most important species of jumping spiders is probably *Phidippus audax,* because in can be mistaken for the Black Widow. These spiders are 1/8"-3/4" long with robust, relatively short legs, and are mostly black with white or red markings on the dorsal surface of the abdomen. Another species—*Phidippus formosus*—has been reported to bite, but the small amount of venom secreted causes only mild irritation, e.g., localized swelling and sensitivity. They are beneficial because they hunt and pounce on flies and other insect pests and eat them. They like sunny areas and are often found on porches or on walls.

Wolf spiders (Lycoside - *Lycosa spp*)

Wolf spiders are robust and agile hunting spiders with excellent eyesight. They occasionally enter homes and garages and can be found almost anywhere inside. They measure from 1/2"-2" in length, depending on the species, and are hairy, grayish or brown, with various markings on the back. The female can be seen carrying around her egg sac and then her babies on her back. Wolf spiders are not dangerous at all but will bite like any spider if squeezed or mishandled.

Tarantulas (Theraphosidae)

Tarantulas are very large hunting spiders. You often see the males crossing the road after a rain, when they are looking for females to mate with. Although tarantulas are fearsome looking, they are not at all dangerous. A large one can deliver a painful bite if molested, but they are not lethal.

In the Americas the term "tarantula" refers to any of about 300 species of primitive spiders with poor eyesight. About 30 species occur in the United States. Many are among the largest of all spiders, weighing 2-3 oz. and with a 10" leg spread. The term "tarantula" is derived from a city in Italy and actually belongs to a wolf spider of that area, *Lycosa tarentula*. Immigrants who saw the big American spiders called them tarantulas. Female tarantulas have been known to live up to 25 years in captivity, while males only live for a year after they reach maturity.

TICKS (ACARINA)

Ticks are not insects. They are arachnids belonging to the group mites. They are bigger than all other mites and they are very important. There are hundreds of species of ticks in the world and they are capable of spreading more than 65 diseases, many of them serious. Lyme disease, Rocky Mountain spotted fever, Colorado tick fever, and tularemia are but a few. If someone made a list of the top ten most dangerous pests, ticks would be close to the top of the list. For some reason, they receive almost no attention compared to bed bugs which, again, are absolutely harmless. Ticks mostly feed on the blood of warm-blooded animals, but some species feed on reptiles. They can be found in lawns, yards with trees and shrubs and, occasionally, inside homes. They prefer the shaded areas of your yard.

If you find a tick imbedded in your pet or on another person or on yourself, do not yank it off. Gently pull the tick straight off with a pair of tweezers. You can also put some diatomaceous earth on the tick and it will come off by itself. Make sure you save the tick so you can get it identified. You want to know what diseases, if any, it can cause. Mark the date of your bite on a calendar and if you develop unusual symptoms in about two weeks, contact your medical professional.

When you have ticks in your yard, here is one way to get control of them. Take a large piece of flannel cloth and tie it to a stick. Drag it through the entire yard, slowly, paying particular attention to shady areas. Any ticks you drag the cloth over will get snagged. When you are done, put the cloth in a burn barrel and burn it or seal it in a trash bag and take it immediately to the dump. Then get some food grade diatomaceous earth and spread it all over the shady areas including along the sides of the house. Get some all along the foundation where there is dirt abutting the house. Then get some Vaseline and put it on all the outside window sills. If Vaseline is too messy you can use duct tape sticky side up. It takes 30 to 40 days for tick eggs to hatch, so you should repeat this entire process in a month and then again one month later. If ticks are in your house, you need to treat all the areas where they can hide. This would be behind baseboards, moldings, and in furniture and carpets, as well as around window sills. You can treat these areas with food-grade diatomaceous earth, baking soda, talcum powder or spray them with Greenbug for Indoors. All of these products will be safe for you and your family and pets but will kill the ticks.

Most of the ticks listed below are only found in the woods and remote areas and won't infest your homes. I am listing them because they can be serious vectors of disease if you should encounter them.

Talaje soft ticks (*Ornithodoros talaje*)

Feeds on humans, rodents, pigs, cattle, and horses. It has a very painful bite, and is found in Arizona, California, Nevada, and New Mexico

Medical: Can transmit tick-borne relapsing fever in some areas.

Herm's soft ticks (*Ornithodoros hermsi*)

Found in Washington, Oregon, Idaho, California, Nevada, Colorado, Utah and Arizona

Medical: Primary vector of tick-borne relapsing fever spirochetes in these areas.

Relapsing fever ticks (Argasidae - *Ornithodoros turicata*)

Feeds on kangaroo rats, rabbits, sheep, cattle, horses, pigs, humans, rattlesnakes, and turtles. It is found in New Mexico, Arizona, Colorado, Utah and California.

Medical: May produce intense irritation and swelling at the bite site in humans. Also produces relapsing fever spirochetes.

Pajaorella ticks (Argasidae - *Ornithodoros coriaceus*)

This tick has a very painful bite. There are many tales about the seriousness of the bite and it is feared like a rattlesnake in parts of Mexico. It feeds on humans, deer, and swallows.

Lone star ticks (Ixodidae - *Amblyomma americanum*)

The female Lone star tick has a star-shaped marking on its back, hence the name. Found from Texas, through the south-central midwest states to the east coast.

Medical: Rocky Mountain spotted fever, ehrlichiosis, tularemia and STARI (Southern Tick Associated Rash Illness).

Gulf coast ticks (Ixodidae - *Amblyomma maculatum*)

The larvae feed on birds and rodents, while the adults feed on deer and other large mammal. It is found along the Atlantic coast the Gulf of Mexico.

Medical: It can transmit a form of Rocky Mountain spotted fever as well as canine hepatozoonosis

Rocky Mountain wood ticks (Ixodidae - *Dermacentor andersoni*)

Rocky Mountain wood tick immatures feed on rodents and rabbits. Adults feed on cattle, sheep, deer, humans, and other large mammals. They are found from the western counties of Nebraska and the Black Hills of South Dakota to the Cascade and Sierra Nevada Mountains, and from northern Arizona and northern New Mexico in the United States to British Columbia, Alberta, and Saskatchewan in Canada.

Medical: Rocky mountain spotted fever, tick paralysis and tularemia.

Pacific coast ticks (Ixodidae - *Dermacentor occidentalis*)

Immatures feed on small mammals; the adults feed on larger domestic animals, deer and humans. This tick is found in Oregon and California.

Medical: Rocky Mountain spotted fever, tularemia, bovine anaplasmosis, Colorado tick fever, 364D Rickettsiosis.

American dog ticks (Ixodidae - *Dermacentor variabilis*)

American dog tick immatures feed on small mammals, preferably rodents. Adults feed on domestic dogs and will readily bite humans. Found throughout the eastern portion of the country as well as in Idaho, Oregon, Washington and California.

Medical: Rocky Mountain spotted fever pathogen and bacterium causing tularemia. It may cause canine paralysis and bovine anaplasmosis and tick paralysis.

Black-legged ticks (Ixodidae - *Ixodes* spp.)

The female black-legged tick is red and brown, while the male is much darker. They are also known as deer ticks and bear ticks. Immatures feed on various small mammals, birds and lizards. Adults feed on the large mammals such as deer, elk and bears. They will bite humans. The western black-legged tick

(*Ixodes pacificus*) is found in Washington, Oregon, California, Idaho, Nevada and Utah. The eastern black-legged tick

(*Ixodes scapularis*) is found throughout much of the eastern United States.

Medical: Both black-legged ticks can transmit Lyme disease as well as anasplasmosis and babesiosis

Brown dog ticks (Ixodidae - *Rhipicephalus sanguineus*)

Brown dog ticks are found worldwide, mostly in warmer areas. They are small and reddish-brown in color. Females can lay up to 5000 eggs, depending on the amount of blood consumed. Immatures feed on a variety of animals. Adults feed on domestic dogs and occasionally humans.

Medical: In dogs, can transmit canine ehrlichiosis and canine babesia. It has recently been identified as a reservoir for Rocky Mountain spotted fever in the southwest.

CHAPTER SIXTEEN

PEST-PROOFING YOUR HOME

The purpose of pest-proofing your home is to keep cockroaches, ants, scorpions, centipedes, spiders, rodents and other pests out. It will also protect you from having to hire a pest control company, which will spray pesticides all around and in your home. Along with pest proofing your house, remember to keep your sink, tub, and floor drains closed at night. This will prevent cockroaches from coming up the drains from the sewer system or septic tank. If you don't have a drain cover, you can fill a Ziploc bag with water and place it over the drain. That will keep the roaches out.

The first step to pest-proofing is to install door sweeps on all outside doors that need them. If you can slide a piece of paper under a door, it needs a door sweep. Also add a door sweep to a door going into the garage.

Don't leave any debris laying around the house. This is a good hiding place for cockroaches, scorpions, and centipedes. If you have firewood, stack it away from the house, as it will attract black widows.

Branches touching the house or roof will allow acrobat ants and carpenter ants access. Trim them back to keep them from touching the roof during the warmer months. Also, sweep down any spider webs anywhere around the outside of the house.

When you analyze your garage door, you will probably find that it doesn't close tightly and never will. There are almost always small areas at either side of the door when any insect or rodent can get in. As mentioned earlier, make sure there are door sweeps on the door from the garage that enters the house.

Put Niban Bait in any areas behind storage or shelves where roaches can hide. Niban will last three or four months, so you only need to apply it a couple of times a year. Niban is made from boric acid and is perfectly safe.

This procedure will prevent most crawling insects and other arthropods from getting into your home. Keep anything that pests can hide in or under away from your house and don't leave outside lights on any longer than necessary, as insects are attracted to them.

You still may get yellowjackets, wasps, or other pests outside that will require the help of a pest management professional. Check your home every few months to make sure all of the work you did is still in place and effective. If it's not, rinse and repeat the previous steps as necessary.

CHAPTER SEVENTEEN

LAWN AND ORNAMENTAL GARDEN PEST MANAGEMENT

You can prevent pests in many cases by treating the soil around your garden plants with food-grade diatomaceous earth, ground pepper, talcum powder, Comet Cleanser, or Tide laundry soap. Very few insects will crawl through any of those materials.

It is helpful to monitor your plants to see what pests may be present. If you have a night light in the area it may attract some potential pest beetles and moths; you might not otherwise know of their presence until they do damage to your garden. You can put yellow sticky traps in various parts of your yards which will attract various pest insects. I have had good luck using bright yellow, stiff paper and coating it with petroleum jelly. A white bucket filled with water and a cup of liquid soap to destroy the surface tension will also attract some pests and they will drown in the bucket.

Spraying infested plants with a mixture of half water and half isopropyl alcohol, mixed with a dash of dish soap, will also kill many insect pests. Make sure to test this product, and others mentioned, on a few leaves of any plants first to check for sensitivity, so they aren't negatively affected.

If your garden is still being destroyed by pests, you can put pieces of flat boards, about a foot by two feet, on the ground in various places in your garden. Many pests will use these boards to hide and you can find them in the morning and take note of what you're dealing with and the necessary steps to deter their damage.

Here are some other recipes you may want to try. Some of them are recommended for certain pests listed below.

A) If you have mites, try mixing 4 tablespoons of buttermilk with a cup of all-purpose flour and a gallon of water.

B) Crush 3 oz. of garlic cloves and mix with 1 oz. of mineral oil. Let this mixture stand overnight, then strain. Mix 1 teaspoon of fish oil and one tablespoon of castile soap with a quart of water. Slowly combine the garlic mix with the fish oil mix. Then mix two tablespoons of this mixture with a pint of water in a sprayer. This is also effective on mites.

C) For most insects, you can mix ½ cup of Tabasco sauce with one onion and a half dozen cloves of garlic in a blender with 2 cups of water. Blend the material and let it stand for 24 hours. Then add two more cups of water and a tablespoon of liquid dishwashing soap.

D) It may be easier to mix one tablespoon of a mild dish soap plus one teaspoon of a vegetable cooking oil with one quart of water. This can be sprayed on all plants. Remember to spray both the top and the underside of the leaves.

You can mix 1 cup of flour with ½ cup of salt for caterpillars. Make sure you mist the plants before applying the flour/salt powder.

Some of these remedies are mentioned in the text on certain species, but most of them can be used on all pests, unless otherwise noted.

CHAPTER EIGHTEEN

LAWN AND GARDEN BUGS
AND OTHER POTENTIAL PESTS

The list of pests below certainly doesn't include all known garden/lawn pests. I tried to include the ones the home-owner will most likely encounter in their garden. There are certainly some that may show up that aren't on this list. If so, I would recommend treatment methods that would be the same for closely related species.

MOLLUSKS

Snails (Helicidae) and Slugs (Limacidae)

Snails and slugs are terrestrial mollusks. Snails have shells while slugs do not. There are a great many species, but only a few are pests in gardens. They will feed on a wide variety of plants and are most active at night or after rains. They often leave large, jagged holes in the leaves of plants they are feeding on.

The best method of control is to put DE under and around all plants you want to protect, as they will not crawl over it. You can also trap them with small pans of beer in the yard. The good news is the beer will also attract and kill any cockroaches in the yard. Never use a commercial snail bait that contains methaldehyde, as this is very dangerous to dogs.

CRUSTACEANS

Sowbugs (Porcellionidae) and Pillbugs (Armadillidiidae)

Sowbugs and pillbugs, which are also called woodlice, are crustaceans, not insects. They require a lot of moisture where they live. Sowbugs (*Porcellio laevis*) and Pillbugs (*Armadillium vulgare*) are actually beneficial as they are excellent decomposers. Pillbugs can roll up into a ball when threatened. My son use to call them baseball bugs. Sowbugs cannot roll up into a ball.

They aren't major pests, but will damage bean sprouts. They can be kept away from plants by putting DE on the ground around the base of the plants.

INSECTS

Springtails (Collembola)

Springtails are very small, wingless insects. Some are brown or gray, while other are brightly colored. They have a structure (furcula) on their underside that enables them to jump when suddenly straightened out.

Springtails are probably the most abundant non-social insect on the planet. There are approximately 650 species in the United States alone and they are found in both the Arctic and Antarctic. They can be very common in damp, organic soil where they feed on fungus. Large numbers in any area will show that the soil is healthy. They rarely cause any damage to plants, but will occasionally feed on young shoots. One species, the garden springtail (*Bourletiella hortensis*), is a potential pest in some situations including in houseplants.

Contrary to what some people believe, springtails are not capable of infesting human beings. This is a myth that is often found on the internet.

You can control them by mixing DE with the soil they are in. In houseplants it would be a good idea to dry the soil out to eliminate any mold or fungi that they may be feeding on.

Grasshoppers & Crickets (Orthoptera)

Grasshoppers are primitive insects with a gradual metamorphosis. They lay eggs, which hatch into nymphs. The nymphs molt several times until adulthood is reached and they can reproduce. They vary in size and have enlarged hind legs that enable them to jump.

Grasshoppers (Acrididae)

Grasshoppers are very common and there are numerous species, many of which will get into gardens and feast. They are most troublesome in semiarid areas as they are attracted to the watering of gardens and lawns. They are very common from Montana to Minnesota and south to New Mexico and Texas.

If you have grasshoppers you can spray your plants with formula C or you can mix 2 cups of DE with a gallon of water and spray the plants. Also put dry DE on the ground under and around all plants. If you prefer, you can bury a large can to the top, fill it about a quarter way with water and molasses. The grasshoppers will go in and be unable to get out.

True bugs (Hemiptera)

The insects in this order used to be separated into two orders, Homoptera, which contained the aphids, scale insects and some others, and the Hemiptera, which were the True Bugs. They have recently been joined into a single order, Hemiptera.

Chinch Bugs (Lygaeidae – *Blissus leucopterus*)

Although most of the bugs in this group feed on seeds, some, like the chinch bug, feed on sap. Chinch bugs are common pests in corn, grain, St. Augustine grass, fescue, bentgrass, Kentucky bluegrass, and zoyziagrass, where they cause brownish circular patches to develop in the grass. Chinch bugs are small, grayish-black insects with white wings. They are found in one form or another in the eastern two-thirds of the U.S. and in southeast Canada. You can tell if chinch bugs are present by pushing a coffee can with both ends removed, about two inches into the soil and filling it with soapy water. If chinch bugs are present, they will float to the top. One good method of controlling them is to soak the areas with a mixture of 2 cups of DE with a gallon of water. Spray all the areas where chinch bugs are present.

Tarnished Plant Bugs (Lygaeidae - *Lygus lineolaris*)

The tarnished plant bug (*Lygus lineolaris*) is common in the eastern and central states but is found nationwide. It is yellowish in color with black or brown mottling on its body. These bugs feed on a wide variety of fruits, vegetables, legumes, and other plants, including alfalfa, cotton, strawberries, and most fruit trees. You can wet all the plants and dust them with DE. You can also put small boards, about one foot by two feet in various parts of your garden where potential pests can hide. In the morning, you can turn the boards over best see what kind of pest you're dealing with.

Brown Marmorated Stink Bugs (Pentatomidae - *Halyomorpha halys*)

One of the most serious pests in this family is the brown marmorated stink bug. This bug was introduced from Asia in 1998 and has spread to at least 34 states. They are brownish in color on top and bottom and have gray, whitish, blue, gray and black markings. It is a major pest of a variety of fruits and vegetables, including peaches, apples, cherries, raspberries, pears, green beans, and soybeans. They also invade homes in the fall to overwinter in a nice, warm house.

Since this bug is so destructive, the Department of Agriculture has developed a pheromone that can be used in a trap. In a garden area, I would recommend dusting all of your plants with DE after misting them.

Harlequin Bugs (Pentatomidae - *Murgantia histrionica*)

Another serious pest is the harlequin bug, which feeds on cabbage and related plants throughout the south where it is very common. The harlequin bug is bright orange with black markings. It is found throughout the south and has been found as far north as New England. The best method of control in the garden is probably to use row covers to cover the plant. These are available in garden shops. Misting your plants and then dusting them with DE will also help.

Squash Bugs (Coreidae - *Anasa tristis*)

Members of this family are large, thick-bodied and dark in color. The membrane of the front wing contains many veins, which is easy to see. Leaf-footed bugs are in this family and occasionally enter homes. They are not garden pests. The main garden pest in this family is the squash bug. This species feeds on squash, cucumbers, and pumpkins and is a major pest. It is a good idea to put small, flat boards in the garden where these bugs live. They will hide out under the boards in the daytime, allowing you to find them and dispose of them. This also works for cutworms as they too hide during the day. I recommend misting all the squash or other plants and then dusting them with DE to discourage the bugs. Or you can spray them with Greenbug for Outdoors.

Kissing Bugs (Reduviidae – *Triatoma* spp.)

Everyone needs to be aware of kissing bugs, AKA conenose bugs, assassin bugs and Mexican bedbugs. A bite from one of these bugs can result in anaphylaxis in sensitive individuals. There are about 15 species of kissing bugs (genus *Triatoma*) in the U.S., and they are found in the southwestern states. The true kissing bugs from South America will come into bed at night and bite a person on or around their lips. They are attracted to the carbon dioxide we exhale.

Adults are ½ to 1 inch long, brownish-black, broad, flat, but stout-bodied, with 6 reddish-orange spots on each side of the abdomen, above and below. This bug has an elongated, cone-shaped head from which it derives its nickname, cone-nose bug. The beak is slender and tapered and almost bare. Its wings are normally folded across the back while resting or crawling and not usually noticed by the casual observer. These insects will feed on any animal, including humans, but they prefer rodents, particularly packrats. If a packrat has a midden (nest) near your house, the kissing bugs may find their way inside and hide under furniture, between mattresses, or in closets during the day. At night, they venture out in search of a blood meal, which may become a sleeping pet or human.

The bite of the kissing bug is painless because its saliva contains an anesthetic. People are usually awakened by itching, swelling, rapid heart beat, or other reactive symptoms caused by the bite and not at the moment they are bitten. A full blood meal requires an average of ten minutes, and the numerous bites the victim sees may be due to a disturbance during feeding, which causes the insect to reinsert its proboscis, the tubular feeding structure into a different location. As mentioned earlier, anaphylactic reactions can occur, with weakness, sweating, nausea, abdominal cramping, vaginal bleeding, and vascular collapse. It should be noted that individuals who are bitten often develop a greater sensitivity to the bites. In South and Central America, kissing bugs are vectors of chagas disease. Some people find the bites on their bodies and assume they have bed bugs.

In order to control these insects, inspect your property periodically. During the daytime the kissing bugs seek dark places to hide, so look beneath flower pots and outdoor furniture, especially those that sit nearly flush with the ground. Check your sheds, garage, and under porches. All cracks and openings into buildings should be sealed as completely as possible. Entry into the home does not require a large opening. They are attracted to light, so keep your curtains closed at night so they aren't trying to get to your indoor lights. Make sure your doors close tightly and your windows and screens are not loose.

If you find a packrat nest remove it. Use a shovel and put the nest material in a trash bag and dispose of it. Then treat the area with a safe product such as Greenbug for Outside. You can also put a light layer of diatomaceous earth over the area. This will not only kill any kissing bugs in the nest, but also any other ectoparasites that may be present. What other ectoparasites do they carry? Well, there are 107 species of fleas in New Mexico, and packrats can be host to up to 37 species.

After removing the nests, put some cotton balls soaked in peppermint essential oil in the area to discourage the packrats from rebuilding their nests in the same spot. Hopefully you'll get lucky and they will just leave your property.

Aphids (Aphididae)

Aphids are very small, soft-bodied insects. Some of the adults may have wings, others are wingless. The winged forms have evolved due to environmental developments such as temperature or moisture.

Aphids are sometimes called plant lice and their common names often reflect the plants they prefer. They produce a honeydew secretion that is very popular with ants, particularly *Crematogaster* spp. (nicknamed acrobat ants). Aphids feed on the plants by sucking sap and they can spread viral diseases, cause galls to form and, in some cases, cause the leaves to curl.

One important pest species is the greenbug aphid (*Schizaphis graminum*). This species is a major pest in Kentucky blue grass and will feed on many other grasses. It also feeds on oats, rice, rye and wheat crops. This aphid has developed a resistance to several pesticides. It is found throughout the United States and much of Canada. It is also found in South America, Europe, Asia, and Africa.

You can control greenbugs in lawns by using Greenbug for Outdoors in your irrigation system.

Other common pest aphid species are the green peach aphid (*Myzus persicae*), the cotton aphids (*Aphis gossypii*) and rose aphid (*Macrosiphum rosae*). The green peach aphid feeds on various vegetables including lettuce, spinach, potatoes, tomatoes, and others. The cotton aphid feeds on cotton, citrus, asparagus, beans, clover, spinach, strawberries, tomatoes, and other food plants as well as begonia, ivy, violets, and even weeds. The rose aphid feeds on roses and will also attack house plants.

Many other species of aphids will feed on most garden crops. The best control is to routinely spray the plants with a pressure wash to dislodge the aphids which will fall to the ground and become prey for spiders and other predatory arthropods. You can mix two cups of food grade diatomaceous earth in a gallon of water and spray the plants as well. Another good spray consists of ½ water and ½ Listerine mouthwash. This spray will discourage lots of pests on your plants. This mixture is also a very good mosquito repellent.

You can put some soapy water in a yellow bowl and attract aphids to it, as they are attracted to the color yellow. You can also trap them by putting petroleum jelly or honey on yellow index cards. You don't want to spray pesticides, as you will kill the insects who like to feed on aphids, such as praying mantids, ladybird beetles, green lacewing larvae, Syrphid flies, soldier beetles, and wasps. Spiders, small wrens, and other birds feed on aphids and will be endangered by pesticides.

Spittlebugs (Cercopidae)

Spittlebugs are small, hopping insects that are usually brown or gray in color. They are not pests in gardens, but they can damage some grasses, particularly bermudagrass. They also feed on a variety of weeds, shrubs, and trees. They are called spittlebugs because the nymphs are covered in a mass of white spittlelike froth, which provides them necessary moisture and hides them from predators. The two-lined spittlebug (*Prosapia bicincta*) is primarily a pest on bermudagrass but also feeds on other woody plants. It is found in the eastern half of the United States.

Spraying the areas where they are found with a solution of 2 cups of DE per gallon of water should help keep them under control. It would be a good idea to use Greenbug for Outdoors in your irrigation system as well.

Brown Soft Scales (Coccidae - *Coccus hesperidum*)

Female scale insects are oval in shape and usually convex, but some species are flat. They have a hard cuticle that is either smooth or covered with a wax-like material. Most scale insects feed on plants and some are serious pests of crops. They are not a major pest in home gardens, but there is one species that is very common on houseplants. The brown soft scale (*Coccus hesperidum*) is found in houseplants all over the world. It is also found on some outside plants in tropical and subtropical areas. If will feed on a variety of flowering plants and ornamental foliage but is particularly fond of ferns.

Because of their scale-like body wall, they can be difficult to treat. If you have plants that are heavily infested, it would be best to discard them. You can remove them individually from plants by swabbing them with a mixture of alcohol and water or dish soap and water.

Mealybugs (Pseudococcidae)

Mealybugs are basically the same as scales, without the armor. The females and nymphs are covered in a white, soft, waxlike substance, and suck the sap out of plants. Some species are pests on houseplants and in greenhouses and some feed on crops such as sugarcane, citrus, grapes, pineapple, gardenias, cacti, and others. One species, the rhodesgrass mealybug (*Antonina graminis*), is a pest of several grasses including St. Augustine, bermudagrass, rhodesgrass, fescue and centipedegrass. The longtailed mealybug (*Pseudococcus longispinus*) is a common pest on houseplants.

If you have mealybugs in a greenhouse or on houseplants, you can spray them with Greenbug or use a mixture of half water and half alcohol. Check the mix on a few leaves of your plants first.

Whiteflies (Aleyrodidae)

Whiteflies are small, flying insects covered with a white powdery waxlike material that makes them resemble very small moths. The nymphs suck the sap out of host plants. They are not major pests in most gardens, but the greenhouse whitefly (*Trialeurodes vaporariorum*) is very common in greenhouses and is found in some plants in the garden in the southern portion of the country. The sweet potato whitefly (*Bemisia tabaci*) has a spotty distribution in the United States but feeds on a wide variety of plants, so will eventually be found throughout the country. It will feed on avocados, broccoli, cauliflower, cucumbers, eggplants, green beans, hibiscus, lettuce, poinsettia, pumpkin, soybeans, squash, sweet potatoes, tomatoes, watermelon, zucchini, and many others.

To control whiteflies, you need to spray with Greenbug for Outdoors. Make sure you spray the underside of the leaves. Also use yellow sticky traps near any plants with whiteflies.

Leafhoppers (Cicadellidae)

Leafhoppers are small, often brightly colored, jumping insects. They feed on the sap of plants and can transmit viruses to the hosts. One species, the beet leafhopper (*Circulifer tenellus*) feeds on beets, sugar beets, tomatoes, and other plants. The glassy-winged sharpshooter (*Homalodisca vitripennis*) is a pest on grapes, citrus, oleander, and almonds, and is occasionally found in home gardens.

You can control leafhoppers by spraying the plants with

formula **B** or **C,** or with Greenbug for Outdoors.

THRIPS (THYSANOPTERA)

Thrips are very small, elongated insects that are either wingless or have two pair of wings. Most thrips feed on various plants and some species are serious pests. A few are predaceous on mites and small insects. Various species will feed on grasses, corn, cotton, alfalfa, melons, pears, plums, cherries, beans, cabbage, tobacco, gladiolus, iris, and greenhouse plants.

The western flower thrip (*Frankliniella occidentalis*) is a major vector of plant diseases caused by tospoviruses. Some thrips, such as the onion thrips (*Thrips tabaci*) will swarm and bite people.

Thrips are attracted to yellow and blue, so hanging some construction paper in those colors with a sticky substance on it will attract thrips and they will get stuck. You can coat the stems of your plants with a sticky substance to prevent thrips from climbing up the plant.

BEETLES (COLEOPTERA)

May and June Beetles (Scarabaeidae – *Phyllophaga* spp.)

White grubs found in lawns usually belong to different species of May and June beetles, which feed on the root system of the grasses. There will be irregular patches of yellowing grass where the grubs are active. The adults are reddish-brown in color and are attracted to lights. If you have grubs in the lawn, the best remedy would be to use nematodes, which are available in garden stores. You can also drench all the areas with a spray consisting of 2 cups of DE to a gallon of water.

Japanese Beetles (Scarabaeidae - *Popillia japonica*)

Japanese beetles are large beetles with copper-colored wing covers and a greenish head and thorax.

Japanese beetle larvae are pests in grasses, and are particularly destructive to parks, golf courses, and pastures. The adults will feed on the foliage, flowers and fruit of many different plants and can cause a lot of damage when they occur in large numbers. Japanese beetles in the adult stage can be handpicked from plants or you can spray them with Greenbug for Outdoors. You can treat the grubs the same way as you would treat the white grubs above.

Hoplia Beetles (Scarabaeidae - *Hoplia callipyge*)

Hoplia beetles (*Hoplia callipyge*) feed on the young leaves, blossoms, and fruit of grapes, peaches, strawberries, and almonds as well as other plants. The adults are about ¼ inch long, brownish in color and appear iridescent silvery green in sunlight. Hoplia beetles in the adult stage, like Japanese beetles, can be handpicked from plants or you can spray them with Greenbug for Outdoors. You can also put a five gallon white bucket full of water in the garden. Put a cup of dish soap in it to break the surface tension. The beetles will be attracted to the white bucket and will drown.

Spotted Cucumber Beetles (Chrysomelidae - *Diabrotica undecimpunctata*)

This species is also nicknamed the southern corn rootworm. Although it prefers corn and cucumbers, it will feed on many other plants. The adult is greenish-yellow with six large black spots on each wing cover. The larvae are wormlike and yellow in color. Misting the plants and dusting the leaves with DE will help control them. Make sure to get on the underside of the leaves. Treating the soil around the plants with DE will also help.

Striped Cucumber Beetles (Chrysomelidae - *Acalymma vittata*)

This beetle has two yellow stripes and three black stripes on its wingcovers. The underside is black.

It feeds on squash, muskmelons, cantaloupes, watermelons, pumpkins, and squash. Control methods would be the same as for the spotted cucumber beetle.

Asparagus Beetles (Chrysomelidae - *Crioceris asparagi*)

This species is a common pest on asparagus all around the country. The beetle is about a ½ long, metallic blue/black in color with yellow spots on the wing covers. The wing covers also have a reddish band on their border. Dusting the plants with DE after misting and putting DE around the base of the plants on the ground will help control them.

Colorado Potato Beetles (Chrysomelidae - *Leptinotarsa decemlineata*)

The Colorado potato beetle is found over most of the U.S, and is recognized by 10 black stripes on its yellow wing covers. The larvae is reddish in color with two rows of black spots on each side. It is a major pest on potatoes. Spraying the plants with Greenbug for Outdoors or misting and dusting them with

DE will help control them.

Elm Leaf Beetles (Chrysomelidae - *Pyrrhlta luteola*)

Although this beetle isn't a garden pest, it does infest elm trees which are very common, and they will enter homes in large numbers when it gets cold out. Pest proof your house as earlier discussed to keep them out.

Flea Beetles (Chrysomelidae, subfamily Alticinae)

There are a number of flea beetles that feed on the foliage of garden plants. They have the habit of jumping away when disturbed. They are very small beetles, usually uniformly dark in color. Flea beetles can be controlled to some degree when they are sprayed with Greenbug for Outdoors. It would be a good idea to put diatomaceous earth or ground pepper around the base of the plants to discourage larvae and other pests.

WEEVILS (CURCULIONIDAE)

Weevils are small beetles with a long, narrow snout. Some species are broad-nosed. They feed on plants in the adult and larval stage. This is a very large family of beetles with many species. The larvae of some species cause galls on roots and some species live inside the plant's tissues. Some species feed on flowers, buds, or fruit, and a few will burrow into wood. Here are a few of them:

Carrot Weevils (*Listronotus oregonensis*)

The adult carrot weevil is dark brown in color. They will

feed on carrots, parsley, celery, dill, and parsnips. Most of the damage is done by the larvae to the root systems of plants. This weevil is found in the eastern U.S. The best way to prevent them would be to cover the vegetables with floating row covers. You can also put some DE round the base of the plants. This will work with the following weevils as well.

Vegetable Weevils (*Listroderes costirostris obliquus*)

These are small, gray or brown weevils with a V-shaped mark at the tip of its wings. They do not fly.

This weevil feeds on carrots, lettuce, turnips, potatoes, tomatoes, and other vegetables. The adults feed on the foliage at night while the larvae feed on the root systems.

Sweet Potato Weevils (*Cylas formicarius*)

This weevil is ant-like in appearance. It has a shiny blue-black abdomen and red thorax and legs. The head is the same color as the abdomen. The larvae of this species bores into the vines of sweet potatoes and through the roots, eventually killing the plants. It is found in the southeast states from North Carolina to Florida, west to Texas.

Cabbage Curculios (*Ceutorhynchus rapae*)

This little weevil is black with blueish or yellow hair. It is found throughout the U.S. This weevil is a pest of cabbage, cauliflower, turnip, mustard, horseradish, and peppergrass plants. The control methods mentioned above will work.

Bluegrass Billbugs (*Sphenophorus parvulus*)

These are grayish, brown, or black weevils who sometimes look mottled because of dried mud sticking to their bodies. They have fine, even pits on their thorax and rows of pits on their abdomen. This bug is found throughout the U. S., with the exception of Maine and the tip of Florida. This weevil and related species feed on grasses and other plants. You don't want these beetles around if you have chickens or turkeys. If a chicken or turkey eats one, the beetles will grip the bird's throat or tongue with the spurs on its legs. The bird will be unable to swallow it or its normal food and will starve to death.

Drenching infested areas with a mixture of 2 cups of DE with a gallon of water will help control them. Using an irrigation system with Greenbug would work better. There are many other pest species in this family, including the infamous boll weevil (*Anthonomus grandis grandis*), which is a well known pest of cotton.

BUTTERFLIES & MOTHS (LEPIDOPTERA)

Butterflies and moths come in various sizes and colors. Most are completely harmless, but a few can be pests in the larval (caterpillar) stage. Caterpillars are distinctive in that they have three pairs of legs, but they also have prolegs—short, fleshy projections on their underside—which help them climb plants more effectively. Moths are far more common than butterflies; in North America there are approximately 700 species of butterflies and about 13,000 species of moths.

Cutworms (Noctuidae)

Cutworms and armyworms are pests to lawns and gardens. They are the larval (caterpillar) stage of the miller moths that we often see gathered around our lights at night. There are several species found throughout the United States. The larvae are thick-bodied, hairless, and marked with stripes. They never have spots as the webworms do. There are many beneficial insects that feed on these caterpillars. Cutworms are mostly nocturnal, hiding in shallow holes or under stones near the host plants. They will also climb fruit trees at night to feed on the leaves. One species, the variegated cutworm (*Peridroma saucia*) feeds on a variety of plants, including grasses, vegetables, and ornamental plants. If you suspect you have cutworms, you can put out corn meal. They will eat it but won't be able to digest it and they will die. Also put barriers of diatomaceous earth, talcum powder or Comet around plants you want to protect. Also put Tanglefoot around the trunk of trees to prevent cutworms and other pests from climbing the trees.

Sod Webworms (Pyralidae)

Sod webworms are grass-infesting larvae of grass moths. The larvae construct webs and bore into the roots, crowns, and stems of grasses. They are found throughout the country. Most of the adult moths are gray or tan in color. They are small in size, about ½ inch long with a wingspan of about an inch. The larvae vary in color from green to brown or gray. Most have small black spots scattered on their body. You will see small, dead, brown areas in the lawn where they are active. You can soak any areas where you see evidence of webworms with a mixture of 2 cups of diatomaceous earth per gallon of water.

Also, using Greenbug in an irrigation system will discourage these moths.

Codling Moths (Tortricidae - *Cydia pomonella*)

The codling moth is a small moth that has gray or brown front wings with dark cross lines and a large copper-colored patch. The hind wings are light brown with a fringed border. They feed on apple and pear trees.

There are pheromone traps available for these moths, and in a home garden, that may be sufficient. They certainly aren't in an apple orchard. You can also hang a trap and collect codling moths in your yard. Mix ½ cup honey, ½ cup molasses, and 1 tablespoon fresh yeast in 4½ cups of water. Put the mixture in a gallon jug and hang from an appropriate tree. The moths will go in and will not be able to get out.

Cabbage Whites (Pieridae - *Pieris rapae*)

Imported cabbageworm or, as it is sometimes known, the cabbage white can be a pest on cabbage, radish, broccoli, kale, Brussels sprouts, cauliflower, collard, and horseradish. The butterfly is small with white wings. The front wings have a black marking on the tip. There are also one or two black spots of the front wing and one black spot on the hind wing on the anterior margin of the wing. The larvae are green, smooth and slender, and have three faint yellow lines. Spraying infested vegetables with Greenbug for Outdoors will help. Also, dusting the plants with DE or using a mixture of 1 cup of flour with ½ cup of salt. Make sure you mist the plants before applying the DE or flour/salt powder.

Potato Tuberworms (Gelechidae - *Phthorimaea operculella*)

Gelechiid moths are very small and have narrow hind wings. The larvae feed on many plants that are important, but only a couple will get in a garden. The potato tuberworm (*Phthorimaea operculella*) is a pest in potatoes in the southern half of the country, although it strays north. The wings of the adult moth are grayish with brownish coloring between the wing veins. There are tiny, dark spots on the front wings. You can prevent these tuberworms by treating all of the soil around your plants with DE or ground pepper.

Tomato Pinworms (Gelechidae - *Keiferia lycopersicella*)

The tomato pinworms larvae will mine the leaves of tomatoes and eventually feed on the fruit or stems. The adult moth's front wings are grayish with orange or brown longitudinal stripes. The hind wings are yellowish and heavily fringed. The larvae are yellowish brown early and turn darker as they mature, eventually becoming purple. This moth is found in the southern portion of the country. Treating the plants with Greenbug for Outdoors and dusting the leaves with DE after misting will help control them.

Tomato Hornworms (*Manduca quinquemaculata*) and Tobacco Hornworms (*Manduca sexta*)

Sphinx moths are medium to large in size and are frequently seen hovering around flowers at dusk. They eventually inject their long proboscis into the flowers to get the nectar. The larvae are large, colorful and have a hornlike spinal projection on their rear end, hence their name hornworms. They often have oblique stripes on the sides of their body. Several species of these moths are pests on plants. The tomato hornworm and the tobacco hornworm are both pests on tomatoes, potatoes, and tobacco. The spinal projection on the tomato hornworm larva is black and the projection on the tobacco hornworm is red. Handpicking the hornworm caterpillars is probably the most effective method of control.

Fiery Skippers (*Hylephila phyleus*)

Skippers are small to moderate sized butterflies. They are stout bodied and usually have brown or orange wings. One species, the fiery skipper, is a pest in some grasses, particularly bermudagrass, St. Augustinegrass, bentgrass and even weedy grasses such as crabgrass. The caterpillars are greenish yellow with a granular appearance. There will be small, bare round spots in the lawn where the larvae have eaten the blades. Drenching the area with a solution of 2 cups of DE per gallon of water will be helpful in controlling them.

FLIES (DIPTERA)

Flies are different from other insects in that they have only one pair of wings as opposed to two pairs. The second pair of "wings" on flies are reduced to knoblike appendages called halteres. Although there are a very few other insects with only one pair of wings, none of the others have halteres. Fly larvae (maggots) are legless, unlike most other insect larvae. Flies aren't major garden pests, but a few types may be encountered. Many species are predatory or are pollinators so it is good to know which ones you have if you find flies in traps in your garden.

Fungus Gnats (Sciaridae & Mycetophilidae)

Fungus gnats are pests in houseplants. There are several species, so they can vary in color from yellow, reddish, brown, or black. They all have the same habit of laying eggs in potting soil. The larvae hatch out and feed on fungus in the soil. The best way to control fungus gnats is to cut back on watering almost until the point of wilting. This will kill the larvae. Then put a one inch layer of aquarium gravel on the potting soil to prevent gnats from laying any more eggs in the soil in the future. You can catch the adults with yellow sticky traps, available at garden stores.

Carrot Rust Flies (Psilidae - *Psila rosae*)

The carrot rust fly is found over much of the United States and southern Canada. The brown larvae burrow in and feed on roots of carrots, celery, and parsnips. They then work their way up the plant to the crowns.

The best way to protect plants from these flies is to keep DE and ground pepper on the ground around the base of the plants. This will also deter other potential pests.

Root Maggots (Anthomyidae)

Root maggots are the larvae of what are called, anthomyid flies. Adults of most species resemble houseflies. The maggots are stocky and about 1/3 inch long. The adult fly lays eggs at the base of plants. When the maggots emerge, they eat their way downward toward the root system. They can destroy entire plants if left alone. They will infest a wide variety of plants, including onions, cabbage,broccoli, cauliflower, turnips, brussel sprouts, radishes, celery, hedge mustard, corn, peas, barley, wheat, melons, spinach, beets, berries, roses, and others. The spinach leafminer (*Pegomya hyoscyami*) is in this group, and it mines the leaves of spinach and beets. Some common species are radish maggots (*Hylemya radicum*), Cabbage maggot (*Hylemya brassicae*), Onion maggot (*Hylemya antiqua*), Seedcorn maggots (*Hylemya platura*), and the Raspberry cane maggot (*Pegomya rubivora*).

You can discourage root maggots from laying their eggs near your plants by spreading DE or ground pepper on the soil around the base of your plants.

MITES (ACARINA)

Mites are very small, microscopic arachnids, closely related to spiders. There are a great many species and probably a great many unknown species because of their size. There are several groups of mites that are the prominent pests in your yard and garden. The main ones are the spider mites (Tetranychidae), which will infest a wide variety of plants.

Spider Mites (Tetranychidae)

Spider mites are very common pests and show up on a wide variety of plants, sucking the sap out of their hosts. These mites also spin protective webbing on the plants' surfaces. Spruce spider mites (*Oligonychus ununguis*) are considered one of the most destructive species as they will attack a large number of conifer trees, including spruce, arborvitae, pine, hemlock, juniper, and Douglas fir. Several other pest species include the carmine spider mites (*Tetranychus telarus*), the Banks grass mites (*Oligonychus pratensis*), the linden spider mites (*Eotetranychus tilliarium*), and the two-spotted spider mites (*Tetranychus urticae*). There are many others as well.

Clover Mites (Tetranychidae - *Bryobia praetiosa*)

Clover mites are pests in various grasses, often entering homes in large numbers as they can be concentrated in the grass next to a building. They are pests of Kentucky bluegrass and perennial ryegrass as well as clover. These mites will invade homes, but they do not bite, transmit any diseases, or do any damage. They can be wiped up in a house with a soap and water rag. Treating the grass around the house with a mixture of DE and water will help keep them under control.

Tomato Russet Mites (Eriophyidae - *Aculops lycopersici*

Eriophyid mites are very small, and it takes a 20X magnification hand lens to see them. They are not serious pests, but they can cause abnormalities of plant tissues, galls, leaf curling, blisters, rusts, and other problems. Some eriophyid mites are host specific, while others feed on a variety of plants.

The tomato russet mite is a pest on tomatoes and other plants in the nightshade family Solanaceae. The apple rust mite (*Aculus schlechtendali*) can cause leafcurl and other problems on apple trees. There are many other species.

If you have a severe infestation, you may want to remove your plants or prune the infested part of a tree so the mites don't spread. If not severe, you can spray all the infested areas with Greenbug for Outdoors, which is effective on mites.

Pollen Mites (Erythraeidae -*Balaustium* spp.)

Most mites in this family are predators of other mites or small insects. The pollen mites (Erythraeidae -*Balaustium* spp.) are predators and they also feed on pollen so when we have moderate or high pollen counts, they come out in large numbers. You can see them running around on sidewalks and patios feeding on pollen. They will be found on all surfaces where pollen lands, including lawns. Pollen mites also bite and they can cause a rash. They will enter homes if there is a lot of pollen next to the house. If you go outside and are being bitten, you may want to spray your patios and sidewalks with a high-pressure hose to wash them off the concrete.

CHAPTER NINETEEN

BENEFICIAL INSECTS AND OTHER ARTHROPODS

There are numerous beneficial organisms in every yard and this is the main reason, after your safety, to eschew the use of synthetic pesticides. Some are pollinators and, given the recent downfall of bees and other pollen-spreading insects, we definitely can't afford to lose any of these species. Others feed on decaying or dead plant or animal matter and are important as well. The most beneficial for a gardener are the predators who feed on plant pests.

Spiders, predatory mites, and centipedes feed on numerous pests. While it is hard to think of a centipede as beneficial, the soil centipedes (Geophilomorpha) and stone centipedes (Lithobiomorpha) are very small centipedes that cannot hurt a human or pet, but feed on numerous insects in a yard and many pest insects.

Some beneficial insects include praying mantids (Mantidae), which prey on a lot of insects and even kill and eat black widow spiders.

Ladybird beetles (Coccinelidae), AKA ladybugs, are a major predator of aphids and other small pests. Ground beetles (Carabidae) are large, black beetle that feed on grubs and insect pupae. Many soft-winged flower beetles (Melyridae) are predators on pest species. Rove beetles (Staphylinidae) feed on grubs, insect pupae, and root maggots, and in some cases, aphids. There are also other beetles that are beneficial. For instance, someone sent me a bunch of beetles he had "infesting" his desert willow. It turned out the beetles were soft-winged flower beetles in the genus *Trichochrous*, and they were doing actually helping to control real pests on his trees. If in doubt about a bug, get it identified so you don't kill something that is actually beneficial to you.

The hover fly (Syrphidae) feeds on nectar in the adult stage, but in some species, the larval stage is a predator of aphids. Some true bugs (Hemiptera) are beneficial, such as assassin bugs (Reduviidae), which hide under leaves and ambush caterpillars. Minute pirate bugs (Anthocoridae) are very small and prey on thrips and other small pests. Some seed bugs (Lygaeidae) are beneficial. The big-eyed bugs (*Geocoris* spp.) will prey on tarnished plant bugs and chinch bugs.

Lacewings (Planipennia) are predators of aphids, thrips,

spider mites, leafhoppers and other small pests. There are many species of parasitic wasps (Hymenoptera), most quite small, that will parasitize pest insects and help control populations.

All these beneficial bugs should be protected from the deadly non-discriminatory nature of dangerous pesticides.

CHAPTER TWENTY

VERTEBRATES AND THE HOME, LAWN, AND GARDEN

MICE (RODENTIA - MUSCIDAE)

The deer mouse is one of the most common rodent species found throughout most of the United States. They are 4"-9" long, are reddish-brown in color with a white chest, white feet, and a bi-colored tail—brown on top and white on the bottom. Their natural habitat is in rural and semi-rural

213

areas, where they inhabit fields, pastures, and various types of vegetation found around homes and outbuildings. This mouse commonly invades garages, attics, sheds, woodpiles, crawl spaces, and the general living quarters of homes.

Mice can enter 1/4" openings—or they can be carried inside. They may get in through broken windows, poorly-screened attic and foundation vents, openings through walls created by cable, oil, propane, electric, gas, water and/or sewage services, and through any other openings or cracks or crevices in foundations, walls or roofs. They can also chew holes directly through siding and/or window or door frames.

While house mice (*Mus musculus*) aren't linked to Hantavirus, they are very prolific and very unpleasant to have infesting your home. Under optimal conditions, house mice breed year round. Out-of doors, house mice may tend toward seasonal breeding, peaking in the spring and fall. Females may produce as many as ten litters (about 50 young) in a year. At very high densities, however, reproduction may nearly cease despite the presence of excess food and cover.

Although mice primarily are active at night, some day activity occurs. Movements of house mice are largely determined by temperature, food, and hiding places.

Mice are very curious and tend to travel over and explore and re-explore their entire territory daily, investigating each change or new object that may be placed there. They are very aggressive, and show no fear of new objects. They dart from place to place, covering the same route over and over again. This behavior can be used to advantage in control programs. Disturbing the environment at the beginning of a control program by moving boxes, shelves, pallets, and other objects can improve the effectiveness of traps, glue boards, and bait. Mice will investigate the changed territory thoroughly. This is why (live catch) traps work so well.

House mice prefer cereals over other items, although they will feed on a wide variety of foods. Mice sometimes search for foods high in fat and protein, such as lard, butter, nuts, bacon, and meat. Sweets, including chocolate, are taken at times. Mice get much of their water from moisture in their food, but they will drink if water is readily available. Mice in buildings catch and eat flies, spiders, centipedes, cockroaches, beetles, millipedes, and other arthropods. Outdoors house mice consume a wide variety of weed seeds, grass seeds, various grains and vegetation. In addition, they consume many insects and other invertebrates such as slugs, spiders, and centipedes.

Here are some recommendations for managing mice in your home or business. Keep rodents out of garages, sheds or barns by keeping access to water, food and nesting materials and harborage areas away from them, especially within 100 feet of your occupied buildings. Repair all holes in buildings that would allow rodents entry. Open doors and windows before cleaning areas where rodents have been living. If possible, run an electric fan for at least half an hour to clear out dust. Leave the areas while the fan is on. Disinfect sites where you have seen rodents or their droppings. General-purpose disinfectants will kill any germs or viruses.

A mixture of three tablespoons of household bleach in a gallon of water can also be used. Spray the area and mop, rather than sweeping or vacuuming. The wetter the area the better, because dampness will keep the dust down. Remember that the territory of mice rarely extends further than 30 feet from the nest, and more often is only about 10 feet. If mice are sighted throughout a building, it means that there are numerous discrete locations where you will have to set traps. When using live traps, oatmeal is a very effective bait.

Never use rodenticides for several reasons. First, if a mouse dies where you can't find it you will have an odor problem. Also if the mouse (particularly deer mice) have ectoparasites such as fleas or mites, they will leave the dead carcass and may attack the human occupants of the house. Mice should always be controlled with live traps where possible from a humane perspective. If you have a crawl space under your house, you should have it mouse-proofed.

If you live in an area where mice or other rodents like to get under the hood of your vehicle and chew on the wires, then you should read this. The best way to keep them from under the hood is to get some cotton balls, soak them in peppermint essential oil, place them in little paper cups, and put them in various places under the hood, especially around wiring. Rodents will not go under the hood of a vehicle that smells like peppermint. This works much better than rodenticides or traps, which, from my experience, rarely work at all in this situation.

GOPHERS (RODENTIA - GEOMYIDAE)

Pocket gophers construct burrows under the ground using their strong forelegs, enlarged claws, and even their teeth. Their vision is poor as is their hearing. When the gopher digs, it kicks the dirt behind with its hind feet. When a lot of loose dirt has accumulated, it turns around and pushes the dirt to the surface using its forepaws and face. The resulting mounds are an indication of their presence in your yard.

Gophers feed on the underground portions of plants, but will occasionally come to the surface and pull green vegetation underground. They live alone in their tunnel system, but males will enter female tunnels during mating season, usually early in the year. Female gophers will have one to seven young at a time. The baby gophers will disperse above ground when they are mature enough to leave their mother and often fall victim to predators at this time. They usually only have one litter per year.

Gophers are very beneficial animals. A single gopher can move approximately a ton of soil to the surface every year. Their tunnels are constructed and then fill up with dirt as they are abandoned. The old tunnels contain the nests, waste material, and partially filled pantries well below the surface where they become important as fertilizer. Soil that has been compacted by cattle trampling, grazing and machinery is benefited by the tunneling process of gophers. In the mountains, snow and rainfall are temporarily held in gopher burrows instead of running across the surface causing soil erosion. The mounds the gophers make also bury vegetation deeper, thus increasing soil quality over time. Additionally, fresh soil in the mounds provides a seeding area for new plants, which may increase the variety of plants on a site.

Gophers are also in the food chain and are fed upon by large birds, other mammals, and snakes. Animals such as lizards and toads will often take refuge in the cool, moist burrows.

As much as I am trying to make the case that gophers have a place in our world, there are times when we have to control them. Poisons are available but I never recommend them. Most of the gopher baits contain strychnine, diphacinone, chlorophacinone, or zinc phosphide. None of these rodenticides are very pleasant and accidents can result with other animals digging them up. These products shouldn't even be allowed to be sold in stores.

A fumigant, aluminum phosphide, is sometimes used to

control gophers but it also isn't recommended. Two children were killed by this preparation in Utah when an exterminator used aluminum phosphide to kill voles in their yard.

There are traps available that can be placed in the burrows, but they are not easy to use and have only limited success. I have found that the best method of gopher control is simply asking them to move. You can do this by pouring a foul-smelling liquid into their tunnel system. Fish oil emulsion works well, and castor oil is also effective. Since gophers generally live alone, once they move they are not likely to return, so a repellent can be very effective.

When using a repellent, you will have to probe the dirt to find their tunnels. Generally a tunnel will run straight between two mounds and they are normally about 18" below the surface. You can use a metal rod or even a pool cue to probe the dirt. Once you hit the tunnel, the probe will fall through. Then take a long-stem funnel such as used to put oil in cars and place it in the hole created by the probe. Pour the repellent into the funnel and move on to the next tunnel. You can use the same method if you have moles in your yard. Actually, for moles, you can uncover the burrow and bury a large can in the ground. Make the top of the can level with the mole's burrow. Then put a board over the tunnel so the mole doesn't know there was activity. It will crawl through its burrow and fall into the can. Check the trap every day so the mole doesn't suffer. Take it out and release it somewhere out of your area.

There isn't any reason to kill either of these beings if you don't have to. Gophers and moles, like all organisms, are just trying to live their own lives.

PRAIRIE DOGS (RODENTIA – SCUIRIDAE – *CYNOMYS* SPP.)

Prairie dogs are beautiful animals, and are absolutely harmless. They live in little villages and mind their own business, don't destroy any crops, and don't carry any diseases—even though they're constantly blamed for spreading the plague. In reality, plague fleas (genus *Oropsylla*) can live on other animals such as squirrels, pack rats, and other rodents and even breed in their burrows.

But when plague fleas get into prairie dog villages, they kill all the prairie dogs. Rest assured, if you have a colony of prairie dogs near your home, they're healthy and do not have plague fleas. That is a myth perpetuated by people who don't know any better or just want to kill them.

People also claim destroying their colonies saves ranchers' and farmers' horses and cattle from breaking their legs in prairie dog holes. This is another myth. Horses and cattle both watch where they are walking and can easily avoid prairie dog burrows. It is only when they are chased by someone or ridden fast by someone who didn't check the area that an accident will happen. It's not the prairie dogs' fault—the blame lies solely with the person chasing or riding the horses too fast in uncharted areas.

Prairie dogs are smart and can vocalize different sounds, identifying many of the animals who stalk them. They have one of the most sophisticated of all animal languages. They recognize hawks, eagles, coyotes, snakes, and humans. Their other predators kill them for food, which is, for better or worse, the way nature is set up. On the other hand, humans—the supposed 'enlightened' species—kill them for fun and profit.

Prairie dogs like to socialize and constantly visit other prairie dogs, even grooming each other. When two prairie dogs meet they nuzzle and kiss. In addition, prairie dogs share their villages with other animals, including some that are federally protected such as the burrowing owl.

The owl is protected under the Migratory Bird Treaty Act (MBTA). In 1972, the Raptor Protection Act added all raptors, including eagles, hawks, owls and others to the MBTA. Gunnison's prairie dog, which we have here in New Mexico, is also a candidate for the Endangered Species Act, since these poor creatures are becoming very rare due to the unmitigated thrill of killing of them by heartless people.

If you have prairie dogs on your property and you perceive them to be a pest, there are organizations that wills humanely relocate them. This is the only method of control that is justified and that I would recommend.

There is an excellent non-profit organization in Albuquerque that promotes the well-being of prairie dogs. It's called Prairie Dog Pals, and is run by Yvonne Boudreaux and Ed Urbanski. Their goal is to preserve the species and its environment, as well as to provide information and education about prairie dogs to the public. They try to ensure their survival by providing them with supplemental feeding in barren areas and capturing and re-locating them where loss of habitat or human conflict threatens their existence.

They want to preserve appropriate areas of land for the prairie dogs that naturally exist in the Greater Albuquerque area, ensure all counties with naturally existing prairie dog populations preserve areas of natural habitat for them, and maintain public lands which allow prairie dogs and other native wildlife to co-exist with humans and domestic animals. Their website is http://www.prairiedogpals.org/ if you'd like to learn more and support their excellent work.

PIGEONS (COLUMBIDAE)

Someone asked me recently if pigeons are hazardous to our health. I told her that alcohol and tobacco cause more death and grief in a single day than all the pigeons on the planet have since the beginning of time. When I look at the pigeon-infested roof of a fast-food restaurant, I can still tell myself that the pigeons on the roof are far less hazardous to human health than the cheeseburgers coming off the grill.

They are frequently described as "rats with wings". The term "rats with wings" came from a 1980 play, "Stardust Memories", starring Woody Allen. Allen used the term in the movie and apparently someone with a vested interest in misleading the public decided to use it in a campaign to drum up business for pigeon control.

The facts are just the opposite. Yes, there are some diseases that can be transmitted by pigeons, but no more so than any other bird, including such popular pets as parakeets, canaries, etc. Consider what some experts have said about pigeons and disease:

"...diseases associated with [pigeons] present little risk to people..."—Dr. Michael McNeil, Centers for Disease Control (CDC) in Atlanta .

"The New York City Department of Health has no documented cases of communicable disease transmitted from pigeons to humans." —Dr. Manuel Vargas, New York City Department of Health.

"I am not aware of any reported cases of diseases that were transmitted by pigeons in Mohave County."—Larry Webert, R.S., Mohave County Environmental Health Division

So much for the health problems caused by pigeons. These birds do have many glorious attributes, and during World War

I, pigeons carried thousands of messages that all told saved many hundreds of lives.

Pigeons continued to be used World War II, as radios were frequently not working due either to damage or unfavorable terrain which rendered them almost useless. Pigeons continued to fly even through enemy fire, and amazingly 95% of them completed their missions.

One pigeon in particular, named "Cher Ami", was a World War I Carrier Pigeon, one of 600 birds owned and flown by the U.S. Signal Corps. Cher Ami was originally bred by the British Signal Corps, but was transferred to the Americans after the war on Oct. 27, 1918.

Cher Ami delivered 12 important messages within the American sector at Verdun, France. On his last mission, Cher Ami, shot through the breast by enemy fire, managed to return to his loft. A message capsule was found dangling from the ligaments of one of his legs that had been shattered by enemy fire. The message he carried was from Major Whittlesey's "Lost Battalion" of the 77th Infantry Division, which had been isolated from other American forces.

Just a few hours after the message was received, 194 survivors of the battalion were safe behind American lines. Cher Ami was awarded the French "Croix de Guerre" with Palm for his heroic service between the forts of Verdun. He died in 1919 as a result of his battle wounds. Cher Ami was later inducted into the Racing Pigeon Hall of Fame in 1931 and received a gold medal from the Organized Bodies of American Racing Pigeon Fanciers in recognition of his extraordinary service during World War I.

Pigeons continued their valiant service during World War II and the Korean War. The Dickin Medal for Valor—an award only for animals—was given to 31 pigeons in World War II, more than any other animal. (The next closest animals were dogs, with 8 medals).

Pigeons have religious significance as well. Noah thanked God for them and Christ defended them. Doves are widely known as the symbols of love and peace.

One of the frequent questions posed to me is "Are pigeons and doves the same?" The dictionary defines doves as: 1.) Any of various widely distributed birds of the family Columbidae, which includes the pigeons, having a small head and a characteristic cooing call. 2.) A gentle, innocent person. 3.) A person who advocates peace, conciliation, or negotiation in preference to confrontation or armed conflict.

Pigeons deserve the same respect and affection that we give to our companion birds, such as parakeets, parrots, canaries and the rest. When they live on our buildings and deface them, we can remove the birds by excluding them from the area, but we don't need to kill them. The best way to remove pigeons from a building is to trap them and relocate them in an area where they can live and breed without disturbing anyone.

When you trap pigeons, pre-bait the area first with whole kernel corn and then set the trap with the corn in it. You will need to check the traps at least once a day. Once you have removed the pigeons, enclose any open areas on the roof with screening to prevent other pigeons from moving in. Before you enclose these areas, you should inspect for nests and remove any that you find. You can also have spikes, wires or repellent gels placed on certain areas of the roof, depending on the design. Normally this is done by a professional pest control company, but you can do it yourself if you like.

SNAKES

Snakes are our friends and shouldn't be killed, except in dire circumstances. They eat a lot of rodents, rodents which can carry diseases and ectoparasites that can affect people.

The bottom line is—if you leave the snakes alone, they will leave you alone. (I know, I know, I seldom followed my advice when I was younger, but I know better now! Never handle a poisonous snake unless you're an expert, and even then you must be prepared to accept the consequences of your actions. It's not the snake's fault if you get bitten.)

Rattlesnake roundups take place from January through July in Texas, Oklahoma, New Mexico, and several other states. Roundups started as a misguided attempt to rid areas of rattlesnakes, but they have evolved into commercial events that promote animal cruelty and environmentally damaging behavior. Thousands of rattlesnakes are captured and slaughtered, or mistreated in competitive events that violate the basic principles of wildlife management and humane treatment of animals.

No other wild animal in the United States is as extensively exploited and traded without regulation or oversight as the rattlesnake. Rattlesnakes are important to the ecosystem. They prey on rodents, keeping the populations naturally in check, which in turn helps prevent crop damage and the spread of diseases such as Hantavirus.

Rattlesnakes are also important prey for raptors and other animals.

Organizers often attempt to legitimize roundups by claiming that they provide a supply of venom for antivenin, but their venom collection methods do not meet the strict guidelines required by the U.S. Food and Drug Administration. No U.S. producer of antivenin would knowingly purchase venom collected at rattlesnake roundups. Rather than add to the nation's supply of antivenin, roundups deplete it by encouraging behavior that leads to snake bites.

Many rattlesnake handlers and roundup organizers attempt to influence public perceptions about snakes with negative misinformation such as false bite statistics. Rattlesnake handlers typically promote their acts as "safety talks" or other sorts of public education. What the public actually sees, however, are demonstrations of extremely unsafe practices, which audience members may try later on their own. Permanent disfigurement or even death could result from the bite of a mishandled and scared snake.

Rattlesnake roundups are among the most deliberately cruel public events existing today in the United States. Collection methods include spraying gasoline into the snakes' hiding places and using poles tipped with fishhooks to extract snakes. Roundups end with grotesque scenes of public slaughter.

In between collection and death, snakes suffer extreme neglect and repeated acts of cruelty. They are typically stockpiled—often for long periods of time—without food or water, and in unhygienic conditions. The snakes may be kept in crates, trash cans, or other cramped containers in which they crush or bite each other. Some snakes die in these containers from capture-related injuries or from dehydration or starvation. Investigators have seen snakes being dropped onto concrete floors from crates several feet above the ground, "putted" with golf clubs while in a coiled position, and made the object of countless other cruel and unnecessary acts. Some handlers sew snakes' mouths shut with wire or fishing line to use them as photo props. Unfortunately, cruelty issues are not addressed in statutes governing the use of wildlife in any of the states where roundups take place.

Where public snake slaughtering continues, children receive confusing and disturbing messages. At one roundup, handlers in the slaughtering area allowed children to touch the tails of restrained rattlesnakes, which were then brought to the block for decapitation. The handlers then displayed the still-beating hearts of the snakes to the children. One handler proudly pointed out how the still-conscious heads of the snakes continued to attempt to crawl away or bite, and made comments such as, "He's too stupid to know he's dead!" This grotesque form of public entertainment is still a feature of most roundups.

Apart from the fact that displays of cruelty are degrading to humans, decapitation is a particularly unacceptable method of euthanasia for reptiles. Because their oxygen demand is low, snakes' body parts remain alive for hours, and their severed heads retain signs of consciousness, such as pupil dilation, tongue flicking, and attempts to bite in response to torment from handlers. Western diamondback rattlesnake heads have been know to retain consciousness for up to 65 minutes after decapitation.

We have already seen some changes due to shifting public attitudes. Over the years, particularly at roundups in Georgia, Oklahoma, Texas, and parts of Alabama, public displays of cruelty have declined. Discontinued practices include stomping contests—in which a rattlesnake is placed in a potato sack and the number of boot stomps necessary to kill it are counted—and rattlesnake shoots, in which spectators test their marksmanship on live snakes.

In Georgia and Alabama, the number of snakes at roundups is decreasing due to a declining rattlesnake population, the discontinuation of public slaughtering and daredevil shows, and changes in the relationship of roundups and the trade in rattlesnake parts. Clearly, as people shun public displays of cruelty at roundups, organizers will reduce or eliminate them to protect the commercial aspects of the event—the trade in skins and the profits from large crowds. However, although doing away with public displays of cruelty is important, it will do little to reverse the ecologically destructive commercialization of rattlesnakes.

CHAPTER TWENTY-ONE

SAFE PRODUCTS FOR USE IN PEST REDUCTION

Here is a list of some products you find around the house or that you can easily purchase that will help you manage your pest problems. There are many others, but these may be the easiest to find and use.

Aspartame

Aspartame is the ingredient in Equal and NutraSweet, two artificial sweeteners. I am not sure I would consider this material safe, but we ingest it regularly if we use artificial sweeteners. In the 1970s the FDA refused to approve aspartame for human consumption due to studies linking it to brain tumors and neurological disorders. Some politicians pulled some strings and it was approved by the FDA.

You can mix a couple of packets of Equal in a glass of fruit juice to control yellowjackets.

Baking Soda

Baking soda or sodium bicarbonate is a mined alkaline mineral. When it is eaten by insects it releases carbon dioxide bubbles that are fatal. A paste made from baking soda will also give quick relief to an insect sting. You can sprinkle baking soda around your home inside and out and around pet food dishes. It will repel ants and roaches. If your dog gets sprayed by a skunk, you can bathe him/her in a tub of warm water with a cup of lemon juice and a box of baking soda with a ½ cup of shampoo. That should neutralize the odor.

Beer

Believe it or not, beer is very effective at controlling some pests. If you soak a rag in beer and put it in the middle of your garage floor at night, it will be covered in drunken cockroaches the next morning waiting for you to dispatch them. You can put some pie pans filled with beer around your home and they will attract and catch a lot of roaches who will drown in the beer. And they don't check IDs. (Bugman humor.)

Borax / Boric Acid

Borax is a combination of sodium, boron and oxygen and is mined from the soil. Boric acid is a crystalline material made from borax. 20 Mule Team Borax is very effective in controlling a wide variety of insects.

Boric acid is a powder that removes the waxy coating on the exterior of the insect's body when they crawl over it. The waxy coating is used to retain water and without it the insect quickly dies from dehydration. When mixed in baits it can control ants, cockroaches and some other insects. The insects also ingest the material while grooming and subsequently die. Boric acid will remain effective indefinitely in a dry environment. Boric acid can be mixed with any food the roaches or ants are eating including peanut butter, jelly, sugar, syrup or honey. You can mix it in ground hamburger meet to control wasps.

While boric acid doesn't cause cancer, birth defects, allergies or other ailments that pesticides can cause, it should not be taken internally as it is toxic if eaten. Keep any baits you make out of the reach of children and pets.

Catnip

Catnip will not only repel insects such as cockroaches, ants, mosquitoes, and others, but it will prevent rabbits, deer and squirrels from eating plants sprayed with it.

Diatomaceous Earth

I frequently recommend using diatomaceous earth (DE) for controlling a variety of pests. If you use this product, be sure it is food-grade quality. Diatomaceous earth is mined from the fossilized silica shell remains of microscopic diatoms. Diatoms are animals that are related to crustaceans of today. They produced shells that are now ground up and used as a powder or dust for insect control. Diatomaceous earth absorbs the waxy layer on the surface of insect skins, causing the insect to desiccate (dry out). Diatomaceous earth also effectively controls slugs and snails.

This least-toxic insecticide is considered harmless to humans and is used in stored grains. Mix ¼ cup of food-grade DE in a gallon of vinegar and spray pests with the mix or pour into ant mounds as a drench. You can make a very good pest barrier by applying Tanglefoot or petroleum jelly to the area, e.g., trunks of trees, and then lightly dusting the adhesive with food-grade DE. Do not buy or use DE sold for swimming pool filters. This form is not effective as an insecticide and, when inhaled, can cause silicosis, a deadly lung disease. Diatomaceous earth is abrasive to lung and eyes—so use proper personal protection when using this product.

Garlic Oil

Garlic is very effective in killing and repelling insects. Simmer about a dozen finely chopped cloves of garlic in cooking oil for about an hour, cool, strain it and spray your plants. It will work on many plant pests including whiteflies, thrips, spider mites, grasshoppers, leafhoppers and aphids.

Rosemary

Powdered rosemary leaves are used as a flea and tick repellent. Simply dust the powder onto the pet or areas where the pet sleeps. Rosemary oil will control lice.

Salt

Salt will kill any vegetation and is a good herbicide for killing weeds in a sidewalk, along a fence or similar areas. Salt mixed with water will also kill snails and slugs. Salt will kill many insects and can be used in crawl spaces or other areas to deter termites and cockroaches.

Soap

Soaps can effectively kill insects because of fatty acids in the product that destroy cellular membranes in the bugs. It also produces a coating on the insect that prevents it from breathing through its spiracles. An effective soap spray consists of 40% water, 40% alcohol and 20% dish soap. You can mix 1 cup cooking oil with 1 tablespoon non-detergent liquid soap as an insecticide. Use 1 tablespoon of this mix to each cup of water and you can control aphids, scales, mealybugs and spider mites. It will kill the eggs as well as the adults of these pests. Do not use it if the temperature is over 85 degrees as it may damage the plants. Sprinkle or spray Tide laundry soap around the foundation of your home to keep ants out.

Sugar

Sugar is a very popular insect attractant that can be used to control many insects if mixed properly with other ingredients. You can catch wasps and yellowjackets by cutting the top off a 2 litre plastic bottle, invert it inside the bottle to make a funnel and put two or three inches of sugar water mixed with a few drops of soap in the bottle. A good ant bait can be made by soaking paper towels with 2 tablespoons of boric acid, 2 tablespoons of sugar and a cup of water. You can put the paper towels in jars with several holes punched in the lid.

Vinegar

White vinegar is effective against ants. Vinegar, particularly apple cider vinegar, will attract and catch fruit flies, fungus gnats, and wasps. You can mix 3 parts vinegar with 1 part dishwashing soap to kill weeds. If you have cats wandering in your yard to go potty, you can spray the ground with white vinegar to repel them.

Green Bug All Natural Pest Control Products

There is a very good commercial product available made from cedar. There are several brands out but the one I wholeheartedly recommend is Greenbug. It has several formulations including one for outdoor use, one for indoor use, and one for use on people and pets. These are available at www.greenbugallnatural.com.

Essential Oils

It is possible to repel and control pests using certain essential oils. This is much safer than using standard, synthetic pesticides. You do have to be careful with essential oils as some people have a reaction to them if it is applied to their skin as a repellent. You do not want to use essential oils on any of your pets as they can have bad reactions as well. If you are going to use the oils as an insect repellent on your body, just add a few drops (5 to 10 drops) to an ounce or two of extra virgin coconut oil, jojoba oil, almond oil, sesame oil or avocado oil. You can make a good tick repellent by adding lemongrass oil to water, mix it well and apply the mixture to clothing in unnoticeable areas, such as the inside of the pants legs and socks.

Here are a few essential oils that are good insect repellents: Cedarwood, Eucalyptus, Lavender, Lemongrass, Peppermint, Rosemary, Sage and Spearmint.

When using essential oils, one way to apply them is to use a pistol-grip squirt bottle. Mix a few drops of the oil with some water, shake it up, and start spraying the pests. If you are treating for ants wipe out kitchen cabinets with a damp sponge and 6-8 drops peppermint essential oil. Then place 3-5 drops of the oil on windowsills, doorway cracks, and in the corners of the cabinets under your kitchen sink.

Centipedes, cockroaches, booklice, earwigs, and silverfish can be controlled by placing several drops of peppermint or eucalyptus essential oil in areas that collect moisture—such as damp basements, garages, and cabinets that house plumbing fixtures.

For mice, place several sprigs of fresh peppermint between pantry items in your cabinets, or make a solution of 2 cups water and 3 teaspoons of peppermint essential oil, spraying wherever you find mouse droppings. You can also soak some cotton balls in peppermint essential oils and place in areas where you don't want mice, inside or out.

If you have aphids or thrips on your plants, you can spray the leaves and drive the insects away with no harm done to your plant.

WEED CONTROL

Here are two recipes for controlling weeds in your yard so you don't have to use dangerous herbicides.

Mix a solution of 80% table vinegar and 20% rubbing alcohol with a dash of dish soap and use it to spray weeds in cracks or along fences. Or, you can mix ½ gallon of Apple Cider Vinegar with ¼ cup of salt and a teaspoon of liquid dish soap. This mixture will kill dandelions and other weeds. The soap removes the protective oils from the weeds so the vinegar can work. These recipes are for weeds only, so be careful as they will also damage plants you want to stick around.

CHAPTER TWENTY-TWO

HOW TO PICK A SAFE AND
EFFECTIVE PEST CONTROL COMPANY

SCARY PEST CONTROL

The problem with the pesticide industry is that a large number of pest control operators (PCOs) are poorly-trained and not well-regulated. Many of them are not familiar with the label or Material Safety Data Sheet (MSDS) of the chemical they are applying.

If a PCO tells you the pesticide he is spraying is perfectly "safe", you may have a problem, as it's a federal violation to make that kind of statement. If he says it is "so safe you can drink it", offer him a glass! If the PCO is spraying your baseboards with a pesticide, it means he doesn't know what he is doing and you need to be concerned.

If you see a pest control truck on the street and it has hand sprayers and other small equipment loose in the back so anyone can grab it, stay away from that company. If they haven't got enough sense to lock up their equipment, they're in the wrong business.

One of the most egregious incidents of pesticide misbehavior occurred in Mississippi in 1996. Two unlicensed and untrained boneheads sprayed 300 homes and businesses with methyl parathion, an agricultural pesticide intended for outdoor use only. There were complaints of foul odors, staining of walls and carpets, and pets dying for no apparent reason. Many residents fell sick with flu-like symptoms. These so-called "pest management professionals" sprayed the walls and floor with this pesticide.

Tests confirmed that the levels of contamination were at least five times the level that requires immediate evacuation of humans and animals! Hundreds of families were evacuated from their homes and several businesses had to be shut down until all the sites were decontaminated. This episode of extreme pest control negligence cost the taxpayers of Mississippi over $50 million and put thousands of people in a very serious situation. Fortunately the people who perpetuated this act were tried and convicted for their crimes. Methyl parathion already had a DANGER label, and is now no longer permitted to be used in the U. S. It was used as a foliar spray on cotton as well as an insecticide and miticide on other plantlife.

I got a letter with some bugs in it from a lady in Alto,

New Mexico. She said she had the local exterminator out four times—at a cost of over $1000—to control them and she still had them. He said they were the larvae of some sort of flying beetle. Instead, the specimens she sent me were actually duff millipedes, a completely harmless little millipede that will shortly die of dehydration once it enters the home. No pesticides were necessary to control it. This fellow tried every pesticide in his truck and failed to control it because he didn't know what it was. The only thing he succeeded in eradicating was the lady's bank account.

There was another instance where one of the major companies treated a home several times for carpet beetles, without success. Actually, they too mistook duff millipedes for carpet beetle larvae. Due to the lack of regulation and low interest level and knowledge of bugs by PCOs, the misidentification of pests is common in this industry. The results can be devastating as to the amount of money spent and the potential harm done to humans, animals, and the environment by pesticides incorrectly used.

Another story talks about a PCO who went out to a house and identified the pest as fleas. He undertook it like a standard flea job, which consisted of spraying the carpets and furniture and fogging the house. He did this three times, and was unsuccessful each time in controlling the bugs. The customer called another company who properly identified the pests as harmless springtails that did not need control. The owners of this house were attorneys, and sued the first guy out of business—which may have been for the best.

Consider the tale of the Immovable Secretarial Object and the Irresistible Pesticide Man. She wouldn't get up from her desk when he arrived to spray the office. (*"He wasn't very nice about it. He just said, 'Lady, you have to get up for a minute.' If he had asked me instead I would have moved...*"). He sprayed anyway, "around" her feet. She was wearing sandals and ended up at the emergency room with welts on her toes, as she was one of the increasing numbers of the population that is allergic to synthetic pyrethroids.

Along those same lines, my sister Linda told me that their company exterminator came into the office in Florida and sprayed the baseboards, and then proceeded to spray all of their chairs! Was he spraying for some kind of butt bug? No one knows why he was doing it because my sister—who's heard me talk about pest control for years now—knew something was wrong with that approach and told him never to return.

During the outbreak of false chinch bugs in New Mexico a couple of years ago, the pest control companies' phones were ringing off the hook. One lady called one of the largest pest control companies in the country. A salesman went out, identified the pest as Johnson beetles feeding on her Johnson grass, and wanted $450 to control them. She called me to confirm the diagnosis. Of course it was wrong as there is no such thing as Johnson beetles and very few people have Johnson grass growing in their yard. She had false chinch bugs which required no control at all.

In another case, a pest control company sprayed a home for carpenter ants several times because he said he found carpenter ant poop on the floor—but the "poop" didn't go away after spraying. Instead, the "poop" was very small beetles that feed on mold, and was present because the homeowner had a plumbing leak that was causing mold. The exterminator couldn't tell a beetle from ant poop.

One time a woman called a pest service because she had weird worms in her house, particularly on the kitchen floor. The pest control operator came out, identified them as boll weevils, and said they would get in the closet and eat her clothes. According to them, she needed the whole house fumigated. The lady was skeptical and called for a second opinion. It turns out they were blow fly maggots falling from the ceiling where a dead animal was being consumed. Now the question is; was the PCO a crook who was scamming this lady, or was he just so stupid and uninformed that he really believed his diagnosis? In either case, that is scary and not what is needed in the industry.

In a similar situation a man was told he had codling moths in his clothes closet. Since codling moths only eat apples, that would only be possible if he had an apple tree in the closet. The customer was smarter than the PCO and didn't let him treat the house.

If you have pets, you should never use pesticides of any kind or use an exterminating service that sprays pesticides in the house. Recently a lady called and told me she hired a pest control company to eradicate some crickets from her home. Rather than use bait, which would be safe if properly applied, the PCO sprayed the baseboards. He ended up killing $2500 worth of her son's snakes, yet didn't kill any crickets. She successfully sued the company.

In another case a pest control (non)-professional sprayed the baseboards in a pet shop. The pesticide was sucked up into all the aquariums and his actions killed all every fish in the store.

There was a pest control company power-spraying around a school in Chama, New Mexico, where children were standing close by waiting for their bus. One kid passed out and had to be rushed to the hospital. He survived, but the company was correctly sued. This company is still in business and has their office in Santa Fe; I can only hope they learned their lesson and are taking their responsibilities more seriously now.

In an incident reported in *Proceedings, Association of Avian Veterinarians,* an organophosphate chlorpyrifos was used in a home where pet birds were bred and raised for six years. The target pests were cockroaches but after five applications, fledglings began to die off, followed by a cessation of egg production. Finally the adults deteriorated and died. The owner realized that this tragedy meant he was also in danger and that was the basis of his lawsuit against the pest control company. The final report read: "The case was settled to cover the cost of the birds and for creating a health hazard for the occupant of the house."

In a case in California in 2001, a person who is now a pesticide lobbyist treated a warehouse with pesticides and didn't post notification. Six policemen responded to a call and had to enter the warehouse. Every single one of them got sick and had to go to the hospital. They all survived, but the pesticide lobbyist was fined $1000. This fellow is still on the discussion boards telling everyone how safe pesticides are for bees and how dangerous automobiles are, as, according to him, they kill more bees than chemicals.

Most of these horror stories that I related to you have two things in common; the inability of the pest control person to properly identify the pests, and a failure to take the potential harm pesticides do to humans, animals, and the environment seriously. Many of them use the Spray and Pray method: if you spray enough pesticides and pray it kills whatever bugs are there, you won't get an angry call back from the customer.

Aluminum phosphide is an inorganic phosphide used to control insects and rodents in a variety of settings. While it is used primarily as a grain fumigant, it is also used as an outdoor fumigant for burrowing rodents and moles. This product is frequently misused.

In one case that recently took place in Los Lunas, New Mexico, a pest control company fumigated a colony of prairie dogs on church property. They didn't follow standard procedure and inspect the burrows for burrowing owls, which are federally protected under the Migratory Bird Treaty Act and the Raptor Protection Act. A witness to the fumigation told the pest control person that owls were present in the burrows, but he continued gassing them anyway.

This fellow was reported to the proper authorities, but because of lack of physical evidence (dead birds, feathers, feces, etc.), he was not prosecuted. I wrote to the church to get their rationale for hiring and allowing this fellow to gas both the protected owls and the prairie dogs. As I've said before, if you have a healthy prairie dog colony nearby, it is plague free.

This pastor's fear of prairie dogs, plus the incompetence of the pest control person, lead to the gassing of federally protected birds if this witness was correct—and there is no reason to think he wasn't.

Unfortunately, in New Mexico, you do not need a fumigation license to gas burrowing rodents with a fumigant. You would need such a license to fumigate a building, a truck, or a vault, but for whatever reason, burrows don't count. It is clear that the man who fumigated the burrows wasn't competent and shouldn't have been allowed to use the product.

How dangerous is aluminum phosphide? It is a highly-toxic poison when the gas is ingested or inhaled. Symptoms of mild to moderate acute aluminum phosphide toxicity include nausea, abdominal pain, tightness in chest, excitement, restlessness, agitation, and chills. Symptoms of more severe toxicity include diarrhea, difficulty breathing, pulmonary edema, respiratory failure, rapid pulse, hypotension (low blood pressure), dizziness, and/or death.

Recently two children in a house in Utah were killed by aluminum phosphide which an exterminator had used in their yard to control voles. The owner of the company apologized for the "mishap". Loss of life is never a mishap, but always a tragedy, and in this case a preventable one.

There was an article in a New Mexico paper about how a pest control company injects pesticides into the walls of homes to control all the pests that could be hiding in the walls. Someone asked me if this was something they should consider. My answer was an emphatic NO.

First, there are very few pests that nest in our walls. Some ants come in from the outside and if they find ample food and water in the home, they may nest in a wall. This would include odorous house ants (*Tapinoma sessile*), little black ants (*Monomorium minimum*), and one or two other species. All you have to do is get the ants properly identified and then put out a bait they like, as described previously.

They will take it back into the wall and kill the queen and colony—pesticides aren't necessary. Who else nests in walls? German roaches in urban/ghetto areas may nest in walls, but the American and Oriental roaches we have here in New Mexico prefer areas with access to water. A wall would be too dry for them to nest.

Centipedes, scorpions, spiders, and other pests may get into a wall, but they won't stay there very long, as there's usually a lack of food and water. The only real pest you'd be more likely to find in walls would be subterranean termites, and the treatment method described wouldn't affect them anyway. It could be possible for wasps to build a nest in a wall, and if that were the case, this method might help. However, even then it wouldn't be necessary to treat all the walls in the home.

Why else is this a bad idea? Well, if the bugs can get into your house through the walls, so will the pesticides. Do you really want someone pumping pesticides into your walls that will ooze into your home through cracks and crevices and threaten the health of your family and pets? Even if nobody in the family gets sick right away, the pesticides build up in your body or your children's bodies and compromise your health. No, thank you!

So why would anyone want to pump pesticides into your walls if there aren't any pests there? The answer is the same as why we sprayed baseboards in homes for many years: perceived value. The industry sprayed baseboards to supposedly kill all the bugs that ran along the baseboard. Of course, very few bugs actually ran along the baseboard. The real reason that baseboards were sprayed was to kill time in the customer's home to make it look like they were getting their money's worth. Most companies don't spray baseboards anymore, although a few still operate that way. Power spraying the perimeter of a house was also widely used, but now is frowned upon as it has no real value and tends to kill more beneficial insects than pests. It is particularly silly when the pest company sprays around your home in the middle of winter.

If baseboard spraying, power spraying, and pumping pesticides into walls isn't effective pest control, then what is? In reality, pesticides should never be used in a home unless you have an infestation of a pest. In many cases, pesticides aren't even necessary then, as one of the natural methods described will work. If someone wants to spray your baseboards or pump pesticides into your walls, ask them to sign a paper stating that they will accept financial responsibility if anyone in your family or your pets get sick from the pesticides. If they agree to that (and they won't), then that choice is up to you. I wouldn't do it without a very compelling reason and a second opinion.

Never let a company use rodenticides to control mice. Rodenticides can kill non-target animals, including pets. And, if a rodent with a disease such as hantavirus dies and you can't retrieve the body, it creates a health hazard. Don't let them use glue boards either because it's exceptionally cruel, and a mouse will urinate and defecate for hours before it dies, spreading the hantavirus.

What to Look for in a Good Pest Control Company

I have said many times that most people can control their own pests without using pesticides or a pest control company, and it's safer for all involved.

If you still want to hire someone to do it, I'd first recommend you find someone who could do it without pesticides. If that isn't available, use caution and get several companies to give you a proposal before choosing. First, make sure they can properly identify the pest you have when they inspect your home. If they are true professionals, they will know the scientific name of the pest and give it to you so you can Google it for more information. If the representative who comes to your home or business doesn't recognize your pest and offers to treat your home anyway, do not let him. If they instead offer to take the bug back to their office for identification, that is fine, and at least shows they are taking their job seriously.

A professional pest management specialist will inspect your home or business, identify any pests, and offer to treat the infested areas safely and effectively. Most companies want to make regularly scheduled visits to your home, and offer various packages based on this. That is okay as long as they just don't spray pesticides inside your home and call it pest control, like we did in the dark ages.

This method is, in reality, simply pesticide pollution. They should come to your house periodically to inspect your home or business for pests, for conditions conducive to pests, and for possible entrance avenues for pests to access your home. If you have a crawl space under your home, they should get under your house to look for leaks or areas where pests can get into the main portion of your home. They should carefully inspect around the outside, looking for wasp nests or other potentially dangerous pests near your home or business.

They should even check any spider webs attached to your home to see if swarming termites are in the web. Pesticides should only be applied if there is a pest present that requires it. In the winter, they can inspect your house as they normally do and also offer suggestions on how to pest-proof your home or business. Maybe they can install door sweeps, fix holes around plumbing, and even trim branches from trees that are touching your home. This is IPM (Intelligent Pest Management).

Many companies—and certainly all the larger ones—have a clause in their contract that prohibits you from suing them. The clause reads something like this: *"Any dispute arising out of or relating to this agreement or the services performed under this agreement or tort based on claims for personal or bodily injury or damage to real or personal property shall be finally resolved by arbitration administered under the commercial arbitration rules of the American Arbitration Association."*

In 1995, the U. S. Supreme Court established that mandatory arbitration clauses could be used in contracts between companies and consumers. Since that time, the clause has been widely taken advantage of by the pest control industry. One of the problems—and there are several—is that it is not free. It could cost the consumer up to $2,000 up front just to start the arbitration process. Very few people have that kind of cash lying around.

My best advice is that if you are asked to sign a contract with a pest control firm, look for that clause. If it is present, cross it out and ask the company representative to initial it. If they refuse, don't sign the contract. There are plenty of pest control operators who do not require contracts to conduct their business.

I've observed three degrees of professionalism in the industry. There are the "antiquated" companies, who still go into homes and spray baseboards, even though they have no idea what kind of pest the customer has or even if they HAVE a pest. Mostly it is old-timers who still do this, those who are unwilling to learn a better way or consider that their way is wrong and even dangerous. In the antiquated companies in the industry, all they know is that they kill roaches and ants. One supervisor told me that there were only two kinds of ants— inside ants and outside ants! He was the service manager. That company didn't do well over the years.

The next level of professionalism is the "mediocre" group of companies. They all have the same habits and follow the same routines, regardless of how unprofessional or outdated their methods may be. I attribute this to a direct result of a lack of training. These folks start companies and develop their methods based on what they did in previous companies that they worked for, even if those methods are no long viable. While this may work for many undiscerning customers and is easy to do, it still puts them behind the true "Professionals", who take the industry very seriously.

Professionalism at the highest degree should be the mission of every company, but it is not even close.

The most common level of knowledge is represented in

the mediocre companies around the country. They use common names for insects that make no sense. For example, they refer to "crazy" ants. Why are they crazy? Have they been to an insect psychiatrist? They are called crazy ants because they run around in circles. Lots of different ants do that. Heck, my kids did that! It's a ridiculous name.

"Acrobat" ants do not swing from chandeliers in the customer's house and pavement ants don't live exclusively under pavement. I have never sniffed an "odorous" house ant, so I don't know if they so indeed smell funny, but I am told they do. I have never met a customer with an ant problem who has squished and sniffed their ants. Of the 48 species of "field" ants that live in New Mexico, only two of them actually live in fields!

In my opinion, every company should strive to reach the upper level of competency and achieve true professionalism in the industry as it pertains to technical knowledge and the use of scientific names for pests.

The true professionals will use only crack and crevice materials in a building, or baits like Niban which work very well. They will treat around the outside of your home using a pin-stream application so they can get the pesticide in cracks and crevices where potential pests hide. They will put Niban bait in water meters as they always have roaches. They will check spider webs they see for signs of swarming termites. In the winter, when there is no pest activity, they will inspect the house and offer to seal any cracks in the foundation, repair any vents, cut back any tree branches touching the roof, and other things they've identified unique to your home that can help prevent bugs from entering the house when spring comes around. This makes far more sense than spraying pesticides when the ground is frozen!

Be advised, some so-called professionals will claim Niban doesn't work. Actually it works very well, but since it is made from boric acid and readily available to the public, they don't want to use it as they are afraid the customer may decide to just do it themselves.

A true professional will post a pest control notification if they are going to treat any commercial account with synthetic pesticides, whether this is a legal requirement or not. They will want to let the public know what they may be exposed to. Many years ago when I was a Truly Nolen manager in Houston, I always posted notifications and it worked great on every level. It had the added benefit of spreading the word about our services, too, and showing potential customers that we were open and above-board. We had a lot of people call and ask for us to come out to analyze their needs.

There is nothing wrong with pesticide notification as long as you are using a legal product safely and according to the label.

If you do hire a company, ask them to give you a copy of the label and the MSDS of any pesticides they use. Read the label carefully. A professional will wear the proper gear as required by the label when applying pesticides. The mediocre and below companies will sometimes not wear the safety gear as they don't want you to think their products are dangerous.

In Summation:

If they aren't wearing a uniform or neatly dressed, ask for identification and to see a copy of their license. Only amateurs would come to your home dressed in T-shirts or shorts.

If they don't thoroughly inspect your home—inside, outside, and underneath (if you have a crawl space)—then call someone else.

If they say they will spray inside your home regularly, send them on their way. You are looking for safe and effective pest management, not pesticide pollution.

If they don't recognize your pest species, or otherwise seem like they are unaware of what they are doing, move along to the next company. I've found that some companies hire car salesman and other types of hawkers to sell pest control, which is not only unprofessional, it does a grave disservice to the clients. Everyone in the company, from the salespeople to the service technicians and managers, should be properly trained in all aspects of pest management.

Choose your pest management professional carefully. Use the same criteria you would use in choosing a doctor or any other professional. Your very life and the lives of those you most love could depend on it.

HOW TO PICK A TERMITE COMPANY

The first aspect of termite control is hiring a competent wood-destroying insect inspector to ascertain what kind of pests you may have. Proper identification of the pest is essential if control is going to be successful. They have to know exactly which species of termites are infesting your home, and not just the general description of either "subterranean" or "drywood" termites.

Different species have different habits, different size colonies, and do varying amounts of damage. If you are going to pay a lot of money to control these pests, you should know exactly what you're dealing with. If your inspector doesn't know what they are, be smart and hire someone else.

There was a case in Albuquerque where a termite inspector walked over drywood termite pellets while inspecting the house. He wasn't familiar with drywoods so didn't make a note of them. It was a real estate inspection, so he was liable for missing the drywoods and had to pay for the subsequent fumigation. He went out of business and the last I heard he was in Alaska panning for gold; I hope he's better at that then he was at inspecting homes for termites.

In another case, an inspector checked a home in Clovis, New Mexico, and didn't find any termites. He didn't notice, though, that there were powder post beetles in the ceiling. When the buyer went into the attic, he fell into the kitchen through the ceiling. The inspector was liable in this scenario as well.

In a similar example, a company inspected a wooden cabin in Cimarron, New Mexico and didn't find termites. The representative somehow missed all of the bostrichid beetles on the window sills, and ended up paying for a fumigation.

Subterranean termites control by professionals

If you have a home built on a slab and you have had a termite job performed recently, you may want to read this carefully and make sure your guarantee is still available. Subterranean termites live in the soil and enter homes through the expansion joint between the foundation and the main slab; or through a crack in the slab or around plumbing that penetrates the slab.

Up until a couple of years ago, a termite crew would drill holes in the slab along the inside of the house and then treat the soil around the outside of the house. The purpose was to prevent termites from entering from the expansion joint or from coming up the outside of the house under the stucco.

Recently, two termiticides, Termidor and Premise, have put out labels that allow the outside of the house to be treated as well as the area inside where the termites are active. They no longer have to drill the inside slab which often involves pulling carpet and drilling through tiles.

This all sounds good, right? Not so fast. All the companies I have talked to that do termite work told me that when they drill holes in sidewalks, patios, and other concrete areas that are next to the home, they use a sub-slab injector to pump the termiticide into the holes. This is contrary to what the label says, and does not effectively protect your house from termites. The Termidor label says:

Where physical obstructions, such as concrete walkways adjacent to foundation elements, prevent trenching, treatment may be made by rodding alone. When soil type and/or conditions make trenching prohibitive, rodding may be used with rod holes no more than 12 inches apart. Exterior drilling and treatment of sub-soil is necessary for concrete structures adjoining the foundation such as patios, porches and sidewalks, to complete the exterior perimeter treatment zone. For driveways, exterior drilling is necessary only around building supports or wall elements that are permanently and physically located at driveway joints. Rod holes must be spaced so as to achieve a continuous treatment zone and in no case be more than 12 inches apart.

I think the label is pretty clear that these areas have to be rodded and the termite folks should be making holes large enough to insert their ground rods. Otherwise they aren't going to be able to get the material to the footer as the label specifies. They are in effect spraying only the top of the ground beneath the concrete slab. If the material would leach down to the footer on its own, there wouldn't be any reason to trench and rod, they could just spray the surface around the house.

Treating outside concrete slabs with a sub-slab injector is similar to spraying baseboards. It is for show only, and doesn't really do any good. The only way to effectively treat a slab would be with a four foot ground rod inserted into the drilled holes. The purpose of getting the termiticide down to the footer is to prevent termites from coming in contact with it and then climbing up the inside of the footer and entering the home. If you only use a sub-slab injector the termites can and will crawl under the termiticide and be able to enter the house.

When you get a bid for termite control, make sure that the representative has determined the depth of the footer on your house. They cannot calibrate the amount of termiticide they will need to use if they don't know that information. If they give you a bid without knowing the depth of the footer, they are using the 4 gallons per 10 linear foot formula. However, that formula is for one foot of depth of footer. If the footer is 2 feet deep, then they have to use twice as much termiticide or 8 gallons per 10 linear feet. This is contrary to the label and illegal. If you have to remind them to measure the depth of the footer, then you probably ought to call another company.

Drywood termite control by professionals

Drywood termites are a major wood-destroying insect that cost consumers millions of dollars in damage and control. One estimate suggested Californians alone spend $250 million dollars a year controlling this pest.

For many years the primary method of controlling drywood termites was to use sulfuryl fluoride (Vikane) as a fumigant. The house had to be wrapped and sealed and the gas injected. It was and still is a major inconvenience for homeowners, as they had to do a lot to prepare for the fumigation as well as stay out of the house at least overnight. It was thought that once the house was cleared that the fumigant would dissipate harmlessly into the atmosphere.

Not the case. A study by the University of California at Irvine has destroyed that myth. It turns out that sulfuryl fluoride is a major greenhouse gas that can last about 30 years in the atmosphere and may last up to 100 years. This study can be found at http://www.sciencedaily.com/releases/2009/01/090121144059.htm.

Another study by the Scripps Institute of Oceanography confirmed Irvine's findings. It can be found at

(http://scrippsnews.ucsd.edu/Releases/?releaseID=965. The Scripps study says researchers calculated that one kilogram of sulfuryl fluoride emitted into the atmosphere has a global warming potential approximately 4,800 times greater than one kilogram of carbon dioxide. That is pretty impressive. In a bad way, of course.

Also, homes and commercial buildings are built differently now than when sulfuryl fluoride was in its prime. The homes of today are constructed much tighter to control energy, and that can impede the flow of gas throughout the building, leaving some areas untreated and containing the gases. This is one reason why fumigation has a higher re-infestation rate than orange oil treatments. Vikane is the trade name for sulfuryl fluoride gas. Vikane is extremely hazardous and carries the skull and crossbones poison label.

There have been other methods of control tried, but most only allow spot treatments. Microwaves, heat, cold and electro-guns are a few. Heat has actually progressed to where it is considered sufficient to control termites in the entire house. However, there is a lot of preparation needed for heat treatment, and the time and labor cost is reflected in your bill for the treatment. It takes six to eight hours to heat a piece of wood internally to 125° Fahrenheit. In addition, the pretreatment preparation required of the homeowner is extensive and, if not completed properly, the applied heat can be extremely damaging to property such as plastics, electronics, and many other items. There has been at least one documented instance of a house exploding because of the heat and propane gas. I can't recommend this treatment.

Approximately a dozen years ago orange oil became a player in the termite control game, and it's a very good player indeed. While there are several kinds of orange oil available to the pest control professional, one brand, XT-2000, stands out. It is the only orange oil formulation that can be used to treat entire homes. The others are good only for spot treatments. Orange oil is unique in that the capillary action of the product works in many ways like fumigation, but without the same risks!

XT-2000 Orange Oil moves through wood like a gas, along the path of least resistance, filling up the treated piece of wood until the termites have no place to hide. Unlike fumigation, XT-2000 Orange Oil treatments are specifically targeted to the area of infestation, so you do not need to move out of your home during the treatment. Because of sophisticated optical equipment such as the borescope, inspectors have the ability to locate otherwise hidden termite problems and treat them. Since orange oil has come on the scene, hundreds of thousands of buildings have been treated. There has been a very low callback rate with this treatment which demonstrates the effectiveness of the orange oil.

If you think you have drywood termites, find a company that uses orange oil to inspect your home and treat it. It is much safer and more effective than fumigating your home.

In Summation:

If the termite inspector doesn't go into a crawl space and/or attic when inspecting your house, don't let them bid on the work. If they don't make a clear and thorough graph or fail to give you a copy, don't use them. If the inspector doesn't measure the depth of your footer, then call another company.

And, if the inspector isn't dressed respectfully, I would recommend calling someone else, too—as he doesn't have respect for his company, the industry or you, his client.

Contacting The Bugman

I Love Hearing From You

I enjoy communicating with my fellow bug-lovers or folks with a challenging situation they'd like to run by me.

If you'd like to contact me via e-mail, you can find me at askthebugman2013@gmail.com.

You can follow me on Twitter @askthebugman.

You can Like my Facebook page at Ask the Bugman.

I have approximately 3500 connections on LinkedIn if you'd like to join me there, too.

And finally, my official website is www.AsktheBugman. com

My current mailing address is:

7595 Faith Rd.

Las Cruces, NM 88012

I recommend dropping me an e-mail first to ensure this is an up to date address before sending me anything via mail.

If you have any pests—household or garden—that you need identified, you can send them along to me. Put them in a vial or plastic container, pack them in a bubble envelope or box, and mail to me at the address above. Be sure to include an e-mail address so I can contact you with the results. Also, please include $10 for this service as it does take time in most cases.

If you are a member of the Bug Club, there is no charge for insect identification.

You are welcome to join my Bug Club. If you join, I will help you with any pest problems you have, as long as I am walking this earth. (If you can contact me in the next life, I'll honor our agreement then, too. Ha!)

This includes any pest problems you might have at home, at work, or anywhere. This offer is open to anyone, anywhere in the world, thanks to the beauty of the internet and the postal service. If you want to join, the cost is $25 for a lifetime membership. You can pay through my PayPal account at paypal. me/askthebugman or you can send a check.

Be sure to include your e-mail address so I can send you the booklet. I hope you'll share this info with your friends, too, as everyone ends up needing pest help at some point in their lives.

I sincerely hope this book has been helpful to you.
Richard "Bugman" Fagerlund

ACKNOWLEDGMENTS

I'd like to thank a lot of people who have had an impact on my life in the bug business. This includes the many folks I worked with at the University of New Mexico, those I met in the pest control industry, and all of the wonderful newspaper editors who ran my columns over the years.

I very much appreciate the thousands of people who have come to me with their bug questions and trusted me to give them a good and thoughtful response. I hope I succeeded more often than not. I also appreciate the many friends I've made through the internet and social media sites, including Facebook, Twitter, LinkedIn and Instagram.

I want to thank Gov. Gary Johnson who wrote the Forward to my second book, "The Bugman on Bugs," for his help raising awareness about toxic pesticides.

I am also grateful to Annjenette Torres with the New Mexico Public Education Dept. for helping me work with the school districts in New Mexico to develop safe pest management programs, and Nina Dewberry who illustrated my two previous books and has developed my website, AsktheBugman.com.

Finally, I'm thankful for my current publisher, WhoChainsYou.com, for getting *My Path to the Bugman* out into the world.

ABOUT THE AUTHOR

Richard "Bugman" Fagerlund spent years in the pest management business, and then 11 years working with the University of New Mexico as a pest specialist, an Entomologist (insect expert), and Dipterist (specialist in flies). He is the co-author of "Ask the Bugman" and "The Bugman on Bugs", as well as the co-author of three scholarly papers during his time with UNM. He wrote weekly natural pest control columns that appeared in many newspapers nationwide, including the San Francisco Chronicle and the Albuquerque Tribune.

When he retired from the University of New Mexico in 2006, Richard went into pest management consulting, and continues to help businesses control pests using least-toxic methods today. He still writes occasional columns for various papers, because he enjoys helping people solve their pest problems without having to use toxic pesticides. He has received hundreds if not thousands of letters from readers across the country.

We hope you enjoyed Richard's book
*Richard "Bugman" Fagerlund: My Path to
the Bugman, with an Earth-Friendly Guide to
Pest Management for Home and Garden*

COULD YOU TAKE A MOMENT TO GIVE HIS BOOK
AN HONEST REVIEW ON AMAZON.COM?

"I'd very much appreciate your feedback. Your reviews
are what allow me to make progress as an author, and a
moment of your time would mean so much to me. Thank
you!"—Richard "Bugman" Fagerlund

Find links to the book on Amazon or at www.whochainsyou.com.

Also from Who chains You Books

FOSTER DOGGIE INSANITY: TIPS AND TALES TO KEEP YOUR KOOL AS A DOGGIE FOSTER PARENT
BY TAMIRA CI THAYNE

Have you ever fostered a dog—happy to make a difference—but wondered why you felt frustrated and alone in your experience? Do you want to foster a dog, but don't know where to start, how to prepare, and what to expect? Have you experienced burnout or compassion fatigue in your rescue experience? If so, this is the book for you. Described as "an embrace from a friend who understands what we all go through; it is a beacon of hope to let other rescuers know they are not alone—a must-read for anyone involved in rescue."

This is not a book about dog training, but a book about people training while working with dogs...*Read more and order from whochainsyou.com, Amazon, and other outlets.*

Also from Who chains You Books

Excerpt from IT'S ABOUT A DOG
BY MAGGIE COUCH

My name is Oliver and I am an owl. I have lived in this great elm tree for longer than I can remember. This tree is my home. I sleep during most of the day, and at night, I watch. But this story is not about me. It's about a dog.

From my tree I can see into the back yard of a house, and I can see in through the windows of the house, too. I can see a lot from my home in the great elm tree.

One morning I was awakened by lots of excited noise from inside the house. I saw the man who lived in the house standing in the living room watching the woman who lived there run around the room chasing something I had never seen in the house before. It was a dog. He was a young dog, with black fur with some white in it.

I have never been a big fan of dogs. Dogs have a tendency to eat birds....*Read more and order at whochainsyou.com, Amazon, and other outlets.*

Also from Who Chains You Books

THE DOG THIEF AND OTHER STORIES
BY JILL KEARNEY

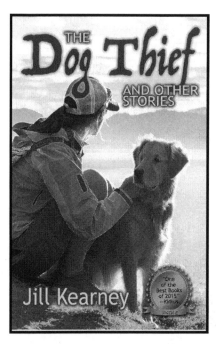

"**D**ecrepit humans rescue desperate canines, cats and the occasional rat in this collection of shaggy but piercing short stories."

Listed by Kirkus Review as one of the best books of 2015, this collection of short stories and a novella explores the complexity of relationships between people and animals in an impoverished rural community where the connections people have with animals are sometimes their only connection to life.

According to Kirkus Review: "Kearney treats her characters, and their relationships with their pets, with a clear-eyed, unsentimental sensitivity and psychological depth. Through their struggles, she shows readers a search for meaning through the humblest acts of caretaking and companionship. A superb collection of stories about the most elemental of bonds."...*Read more and order from who-chainsyou.com, Amazon, and other outlets.*

About Who Chains You Books

WELCOME TO WHO CHAINS YOU: PUBLISHING AND SPIRITUAL MENTORING FOR ANIMAL ACTIVISTS AND ANIMAL RESCUERS.

Animal activists and rescuers find ourselves at the forefront of THE social issue of modern times. The last hundred years have seen major leaps for women's rights, racial equality, and—most recently—gay rights. Even the animals have gained some ground. But, unfortunately, we have a LONG way to go for true freedom for those who remain voiceless in our society.

Often, at the end of the day, advocates and rescuers are left tired, frustrated, and burned out. Who Chains You understands, and we want to help. We are publishing books for and about activists and rescuers—in all genres from children's to fiction to autobiographies.

Read more about us at whochainsyou.com.

Made in the USA
San Bernardino, CA
06 February 2019